BORED AGAIN CATHOLIC

How the Mass Could
Save Your Life

TIMOTHY P. O'MALLEY

Our Sunday Visitor

www.osv.com
Our Sunday Visitor Publishing Division
Our Sunday Visitor, Inc.
Huntington, Indiana 46750

Copyright © 2017 by Timothy P. O'Malley. Published 2017.

22 21 20 19 18 17   1 2 3 4 5 6 7 8 9

Our Sunday Visitor Publishing Division, Our Sunday Visitor, Inc., 200 Noll Plaza, Huntington, IN 46750; 1-800-348-2440.

ISBN: 978-1-68192-058-0 (Inventory No. T1807)
eISBN: 978-1-68192-063-4
LCCN: 2016952291

Cover design: Lindsey Riesen
Cover art: Shutterstock
Interior image: Shutterstock

PRINTED IN THE UNITED STATES OF AMERICA

ABOUT THE AUTHOR

Timothy P. O'Malley, Ph.D., is director of the Notre Dame Center for Liturgy in the McGrath Institute for Church Life. He teaches in the Department of Theology at the University of Notre Dame. He researches in the areas of liturgy, catechesis, and Christian spirituality. He is the author of *Liturgy and the New Evangelization: Practicing the Art of Self-Giving Love* (Liturgical Press, 2014). He and his wife, Kara, live in South Bend, Indiana, and have one son.

CONTENTS

CHAPTER ONE

In Praise of (Some) Boredom

When I was young, my family went on what seemed like an indeterminable number of road trips through Florida. Constantly approaching boredom, my mind would create ways to entertain itself as we cruised past the swampy landscape of the state. In the morning, the rising sun slowly illuminating the Florida Turnpike provided a welcome distraction. In the afternoon, when the inevitable thunderstorms struck, I watched with wonder as raindrops on the windows expanded and then dissipated. On those rare occasions in which we left the state, I delighted in the changing colors of trees and soil that met us as we passed into the rich clay of southern Georgia. On these road trips, boredom was not something to be avoided at all costs. It was an opportunity to let my mind wander through the delights of creation.

We no longer dwell in an era in which boredom is an occasion for the play of the mind. While on the very same road trips that we endured, our children are occupied by portable DVD players, games available on tablet computers, and devices that are connected to the Internet. And even those of us reared before the dawn of the smart phone are taken in by its siren call to escape boredom at all costs. When boredom rears its humdrum head, we check the latest sports scores or our various social media accounts. We escape into the bliss of constant entertainment and, soon enough, the threat of boredom is eliminated.

What happens, though, when we are no longer bored? What art will no longer be created? What novels will remain unwritten? What scientific theories not be explored? Will young men and women cease imagining what it would be like to fall in love with each other, to create a life together?

While the entire human family should undoubtedly ask these questions, we Catholics should be especially concerned about the disappearance of boredom from our lives. Within the Catholic imagination, boredom is not something that is to be avoided but rather is essential to the spiritual life. The Spiritual Canticle, by St. John of the Cross, was composed as he endured the mind-numbing boredom of being wrongfully locked away in prison, internally composing poetry addressed to the God whose voice he longed to hear. With our growing aversion to boredom, it is possible that we as Catholics are losing the capacity to receive such spiritual insight. Or perhaps, even, to pray at all. Spiritual formation should re-form us to seek anew the saving and sweet gift of boredom.

THE MASS IS BORING

Our fear of boredom is in fact most perilous to fruitful participation in the Mass. It often seems that what we desire most in the celebration of the Mass is an occasion to be entertained. We want a homilist who can make jokes and tell engaging stories about his life. We want music that is upbeat, a liturgical equivalent to what we listen to while working out at the gym. We want liturgies that are short so that we can resume our busy schedules. Yet in this desire for entertainment we distract ourselves from the contemplative encounter that each celebration of the Mass offers.

Boredom at Mass is not something that should be eliminated. The moment in which we find ourselves bored while listening to the readings and the homily, bored while hearing the same Eucharistic Prayer offered once again, and bored while singing this same hymn we chant every Advent, is also the moment in which we are invited to participate more fully in the love of God poured out in Christ.

To let our minds be distracted by the way that incense fractures the colored light, revealing the beauty of a beautiful God, or to let our imaginations wander during the homily, may be less a matter of frittering away the time and more often a moment in which God's voice speaks in the stillness of our hearts. To lose our attention during the praying of the Eucharistic Prayer and find ourselves fascinated by the crucifix is not something that should be stopped but is instead our own particular way of participating in the Mass this day. For Catholics, fruitful participation in the Mass requires this ability to let the mind wander and wonder alike.

Our rejection of the state of boredom, therefore, makes it quite possible that full, conscious, and active participation in the Mass is actually made more difficult; for it is saving boredom that gives rise to wondrous contemplation of the Eucharistic love of Christ. Boredom during Mass, in this case, is in fact an invitation to new spiritual growth for the Christian. It is the way God calls us toward a deeper participation in the drama of redemption.

GOOD BOREDOM, BAD BOREDOM

While the kind of boredom addressed above is a very good thing for contemplation, it is often the case that there are types of boredom in the Mass that are not invitations toward deeper contemplation. Lyrics of hymns that fail to foster desire, to seed the imagination with a renewed sense of what it means to worship God, are not "good boring." Homilies at Mass that are disorganized, disconnected from the Gospel, and delivered as if they are want ads from a newspaper are not "good boring." Churches whose architecture has more in common with the local strip mall than those sacred spaces that have mattered to Catholics throughout history are not "good boring."

There is another type of bad boredom that needs to be dealt with. Simply, the Mass often fails to capture our attention insofar as we have not been disposed to receive the Eucharist fruitfully. Those who gather in the Sunday assembly to listen to the Scripture readings proclaimed do not understand them. We seem less than committed to recognizing the gift of Christ's presence among us in his Body and Blood. We remain indifferent to expressing the kind of Eucharistic friendship that is the consequence of our identity as those gathered into the body of Christ.

The reality at many of our parishes is that we often seem to deal with more of the "bad boring" than the "good boring." The promise of the liturgical renewal enacted by the Second Vatican Council is still unmet at too many of our parishes either because of poor liturgy or poor catechetical formation. Yet at the heart of this negative sense of boredom is this: we do not rejoice in the Good News that Jesus Christ is Lord of the universe. Suffering and death are not the ultimate meaning of the human condition—the meaning of the world is revealed in the crucified and glorified God-man who offers to the Father the entire life of the Church as a sacrifice of love. We carry out the Mass as obligation and task but have forgotten to delight in the offering, to comprehend the glories revealed on the table of the Word and on the altar of sacrifice, the glories unfolding in my own life if I only had the courage to see them.

The response we must have, then, to the bad boring is to seek a renewed sense of the power of the Mass itself to evangelize the world. We seem to have forgotten the way that the beauty of the Mass can change not only us but the entire world. How Christ in the Eucharist, through the power of the Spirit, still draws the entire human family to himself and toward salvation.

A LAY PRIMER FOR MASS

This book invites readers to learn to pray through the good boredom, as well as to avoid the bad boredom that distracts us from the heart of the personal and communal encounter with Christ that takes place at every Mass. In the medieval era, Mass primers for laity helped women and men to participate in Mass by providing certain prayers and poems they could read while the liturgy was being celebrated.

While the Second Vatican Council requires more of us during the Mass than saying private prayers to dispose us toward worship, it is still the case that lay men and women are looking to be formed to participate spiritually in the Eucharistic life of the Church. We need to know what is happening at Mass during a specific time. We need to reflect on the spiritual implications of the Mass for our lives. We need to think about what keeps us from participating fully, whether it's bad music or the frenzied nature of daily life. In fact, the need for these books has increased insofar as we are not simply to "hear" Mass on a Sunday, but to participate so fully in the Eucharist that our work, our family life, and our friendships take on a Eucharistic tenor.

Thus, this book functions as a lay primer for participating in the liturgy. It will offer a spiritual reflection on every part of the Mass, grounded in the experience of a husband and father who goes to Mass every Sunday with child in tow. This book is not meant to be read quickly, but will instead provide a personal and communal reflection on how we can learn to pray the liturgy better. The text will be honest, not sugarcoating the difficulties that arise as one learns to pray the liturgy well. It will attend very directly to the distractions that take place at every Mass, especially for those of us who come along with families. It will offer loving critiques of certain habits that the Church has developed in celebrating the Mass, ones that make it more difficult for many of us to fruitfully participate in the Mass. But most importantly, the book will offer a sketch of what a Eucharistic life looks like; how learning to pray the Mass might renew Church and society alike.

This book is dedicated to the thousands of students, youth ministers, campus ministers, and undergraduates I have been privileged to teach at Notre Dame. Like God in the book of Exodus, I have heard your cries of boredom. I know how difficult it is to attend parishes where it seems spiritual vitality is absent. I know the temptation that you inevitably feel to excuse yourself from Sunday practice because, really, no one will miss you. I know how hard it is to convince adolescents—whether you minister to them or parent them—to attend Mass each Sunday (or even once a month). But it is my hope that through reading this book many young adults will come to see—perhaps for the first time—the spiritual riches of the Eucharist. And to those ministers and teachers who struggle to convince these students to participate in the sacrifice of praise at the heart of the Mass: I hope you'll discover in these pages something that will revive your weary souls.

This book could be considered a pastoral sequel to my earlier *Liturgy and the New Evangelization: Practicing the Art of Self-Giving Love* (Liturgical Press, 2014). It is the result of years of teaching undergraduates across the United States how to pray the Mass better. The reader will notice a number of endnotes that, if you want, can take you into the riveting world of liturgical and sacramental theology. On the other hand, if you're happy praying better (and that should be our ultimate goal), ignore the notes. I know that my grandparents, who taught me to pray the Mass in the first place, would pay no attention to these notes. So you would be in very good company.

Still, I include the notes for the seeker who wants to think about God. It's okay to want to think about God. As a public school kid on a bus in East Tennessee, I would read the *Catechism of the Catholic Church* every single day on the way to school. There, I discovered Augustine and

Aquinas, Catherine of Siena and Hildegard of Bingen. I realized that I could pray and think, think and pray. The notes, then, are included for all those other awkward kids on a bus in Tennessee, looking to begin their burgeoning theological career (and perhaps avoid attracting too many friends).

CHAPTER TWO

Entrance

"Lift Up Your Heads, O Gates"
(Ps 24:7)

A Sunday morning around the O'Malley household is the very performance of chaos. Rising at 6:00 a.m., our son demands that we immediately travel as a family to sit on the living room couch. There, with sleep encrusted eyes, we begin to receive the morning orders of our toddler major general. Before coffee begins to pulse through our veins, we have been told to turn on the television so that he can watch *Curious George*. Generally denying this order not because of deeply held principles around screen time but out of fear of being judged by much better parents, we turn on one of Elmo's latest albums, singing and dancing along as the sun pierces through the wintry perma-cloud characteristic of South Bend winters. We also get another cup of coffee. And then another.

Soon after these morning rites, it is time for breakfast. That is, it is time for *us* to eat our breakfast. Our son's relationship with eating in the morning is not quite as committed. At first, the hunger that occupies his whole being must be sated. Then, once food is available, that hunger is no more. He wants to dance and sing again. With us. When dishes are being done and his food is being thrown out, he now becomes very interested in eating not just his breakfast but all the food in the world. And there was evening, and there was morning, the first tantrum.

Now running behind after an hour-long breakfast ordeal, it is time to shower and get dressed for Mass. One of us (left unnamed to protect the civilization of love that we're trying to cultivate in our domestic church) goes upstairs to shower, taking close to forty-five minutes. Another of us decides that he is tired, a bit fussy, and would like to play one game of *Madden 2011* before departing to worship the living God. Losing track of time, the game-player forgets to adequately prepare food and beverages for his son to take to Mass and finally gets upstairs to shower ten minutes before we must leave to offer the Eucharistic sacrifice. In the meantime, our son has now listened to two hours of Elmo's music, is showing signs that he would prefer to take a nap, and is hiding from us so that he does not have to get dressed.

Somehow, we get out the door with six minutes to spare, arriving merely a minute late. We schlep our son, his vast array of Mass needs ranging from food to holy cards, and ourselves to a front pew where immediately the toddler issues his second order of the day by pointing a finger at a door: "Leave!" We tell him no, and then spend the next hour of our lives alternating between participating in the Mass and discouraging our son from treating the pew as his personal jungle gym. After communion, the son again demands to leave, we whisper, "Soon," and then we return to our now snow-covered car with everything in tow (after blessing ourselves at *every* holy water font in the Church). We arrive home, slightly tired, our wills weakened enough to let the sleepy toddler watch a single episode of *Curious George* before lunch and a nap.

In my weaker moments, just as I am about to put our son down for a Sunday morning nap, I wonder why we participate in this exhausting ritual from week to week. Among my high school and college friends—an excellent array of human beings—there are many who try to get to Mass when they can but don't treat it as a weekly obligation. They may pray together as a family at home, which may very well be more relaxing and spiritually illuminating for all involved. But they don't orient their entire Sundays to fulfilling this Eucharistic obligation. Why is it so important for the O'Malley family that we *must* be present on Sunday mornings and holy days of obligation? Couldn't we continue to be decent Catholics by only attending now and again?

THE "CATHOLIC" CHURCH

Of course, after I have taken a sufficient nap to defeat the Sunday morning exhaustion, I remember again why we go to such lengths to pray with Christ's Body every Sunday morning. There are a number of religious traditions in which "being present" is less important than "authentic engagement." Why sing a hymn with everyone else when I prefer the experience of singing alone? Why pray a psalm with the People of God when I get more out of praying in the privacy of my room? Because in Catholicism, joining together to pray, coming from all corners of our towns and villages, is an enactment of what it means to belong to the Catholic Church to begin with. To pray together, to worship together, this is what it means to belong to the Church.

Louis Bouyer, a theologian at the Second Vatican Council, wrote:

> The Church exists only in these assemblies in which men meet one another as "neighbors," who together hear the Divine Word in order to unite in a common faith by celebration of the "Lord's Supper," in which their love, of the Father and their brethren, is exercised inseparably in unanimous praise and charity.[1]

The Church comes into existence fully in this gathering of men and women to worship the living God. Every family and person gathered in that assembly, whether or not they're fully aware of what they're doing, are signs of Christ's glorious body on earth. The Church only becomes what she is intended to be when all of humanity gathers together to participate in the divine praise that is the very vocation of the Church.

Going to Mass is not fundamentally about my unique spiritual experience, but about giving over part of myself in love to all other believers so that together we can manifest Christ's love for the world. Even if I'm distracted by work, dealing with a sick toddler, or more interested in watching a football game later in the afternoon, my presence on Sunday is necessary for the Church's mission of divine love. The Church is "Catholic" because her destiny is to gather all the human family into the peace of Christ's love.

THE ENTRANCE RITES

In this sense, our very first act of worship at Mass occurs even before we enter that assembly. Rather, the moment that we as a family reorient our entire day to participate in the Eucharistic sacrifice of Christ's body, we have already offered ourselves to God. Yet, the opening rites at the beginning of Mass, including the procession, are a preparation for entering fully into the presence of the Lord of heaven and earth. Psalm 24 describes a procession in which Israel climbs the mountain of the Lord, approaching the Temple courts. The Psalmist cries out to the doors of the Temple:

> Lift up your heads, O gates;
> > rise up, you ancient portals,
> > that the king of glory may enter. (Ps 24:9)

The Temple itself must make room for God's presence to dwell in the midst of the holy ones of Israel.

At the beginning of Mass, as the priest and servers, lectors, and Eucharistic ministers process down the aisle, the Church makes room for the presence of Christ in the Scriptures and the Eucharist. The incense that is used at the beginning of Mass is an image of the *Shekinah*, the cloud of glory representative of God's very presence that descends into the holy of holies in the Temple. This cloud of incense sanctifies the assembly gathered that day to participate in the Eucharistic worship of the beloved Son.

The priest also invites us to mark our bodies with the cross, to name ourselves as creatures baptized into the life of the Father, the Son, and the Holy Spirit. Despite the plurality of individuals gathered in our parish, we share in common before all else the sign of the cross, which has made us brothers and sisters of the Word made flesh and therefore of one another.

Thus, The Entrance Rite invites every one of us gathered in that assembly to make a space for the divine presence to enter into our hearts. God is already at work in our lives, wooing us in the first place to join our voices with God's holy ones at Mass that day. God is at work in gathering together an assembly of priests, prophets, and kings. Yet the triune God still wants us to create even more space, to make room for God to enter into our individual lives as we pray together the Church's Eucharistic liturgy.

At every Mass, as we assemble together, God invites us to:

> Lift up the gates of your homes so that I may come
> dwell among you there.
> Lift up the gates of your hands that through them I
> may reach out in mercy to the ends of the earth.
> Lift up the gates of your lips that you may speak
> my loving name to all the nations.
>
> Lift up the gates of your eyes so that you may learn
> to see my presence dwelling among you.
> Lift up the gates of your ears so that you may hear
> my saving Word this day.
> Lift up the gates of your mouth so that you may
> taste the sweetness of the Lord.

QUESTIONS AND PRACTICES

1. Why do you decide to go to Mass weekly?

2. The Church is defined first and foremost by its gathering to celebrate the Eucharist. How might this change the way that you understand participation in the Eucharist?

3. What things might you do over the course of the week to prepare to welcome God's presence in the Mass?

CHAPTER THREE

The Chant

"Sing to the LORD a New Song"
(Ps 96:1)

Among my undergraduates, music functions as a soundtrack to their lives. As they walk across campus, earbuds connected to their iPhones, their pilgrimage to class is punctuated by ear candy intended to either soothe the soul or excite the affections for another day. Whether students (or some of their faculty) are secretly dancing to the music of Taylor Swift or grounded in Mozart's Jupiter, they're understanding their world differently through the power of song.

I came to recognize the interconnection between music and movement while living in Boston during my doctoral studies. On my lengthy walk to class I listened nearly every day to the symphonies of Mozart. Through the power of Mozart's artistry, the world around me began to open up. I noticed the stunning greenness of the trees, together with the shape of each individual leaf. I attended to the architectural fittingness of the homes that I passed by as I traversed the sidewalks of Newton. The external world, once mere background noise to my inner musings, became a gift through the power of a song that pulled me outside of myself toward the harmony of the universe.

The Church has recognized the power of music to give this kind of shape to our perception of God's activity in the world. As we enter into the Mass, as the Church ascends upon her pilgrimage toward the heavenly liturgy of love that is God's very life, we sing. In fact, the Church has found this singing so important that we have been given both words and a tune to sing as we enter into the celebration of the Mass. The introit (or entrance chant) focuses our attention at the very beginning of Mass upon the mystery that we celebrate during this liturgical season. On the Second Sunday of Advent, we cry out:

> O people of Sion, behold,
> the Lord will come to save the nations,
> and the Lord will make the glory of his voice
>   heard
> in the joy of your heart. (Cf. Is 30:19, 30)

Here, we recall Israel's longing that God might act definitively in history. We Christians are to take up this very same posture during the season of Advent, longing for the second coming of our Lord. Already, Jesus comes again into our midst through the joy of singing this song, as the hearts of every believer stretch forth yearning for God's presence among us. This song of longing for God's presence, while especially appropriate during Advent, is meant to inform our desires every time we go to Mass.

The preference for a set chant at the beginning of the Mass is more than a holdover from an "old-fashioned" Catholicism. These introit chants are always taken from the Scriptures. The entrance chant focuses our attention upon the history of presence that God has with the hu-man race. When on the Friday after Ash Wednesday, we cry out,

> The Lord heard and had mercy on me;
> the Lord became my helper (Ps 30[29]:11),

we join our voices with all of Israel, with the entire history of saints and sinners who have benefited from the merciful love of God. God has forgiven the human family before. God has forgiven me before. And at every Mass, God's heart of mercy comes forth to greet his prodigal children.

Of course, few of us hear these entrance chants on a regular basis. Most of our parishes substitute a hymn, one that should have the very same theme as the introit for the day. The problem with many of these published hymns is that they focus too much upon the gathering of the assembly. We end up a singing a rally song about ourselves, about how excellent we are as the Church.

The entrance song or chant should focus less upon ourselves and more on how the Father, the Son, and the Holy Spirit has redeemed the human race, gathering us together now to sing a new song to the Lord: "Sing to the LORD a new song; / sing to the Lord, all the earth. / Sing to the LORD, bless his name" (Ps 96:1–2). We gather together to praise the God who is active within human history, not to feel pepped up or to remind God that he has chosen a remarkable people.

SING A NEW SONG

Still, singing is not simply a matter of vocal performance or entertainment for the Christian. Instead, as St. Augus-tine notes, to sing this new song to the Lord is to commit ourselves to the unity of all humanity that the Church promises. We come into Church with many songs ringing in our ears. We hear the song of war that tells us that the only way toward peace is through the sword. We hear the music of efficiency that reduces women and men to their jobs and income brackets. The orchestra of advertising plays its symphony in which women and men are merely consumers in a world in which happiness can be achieved through acquisition alone.

In the midst of these unsatisfying songs, we sing a hymn of joy that once again reminds us of our identity as creatures made for praise. We are not first and foremost warriors, workers, or consumers, but women and men created in the image and likeness of God. To sing at the very beginning of Mass is to dispose ourselves toward the worship that we are to offer during the rest of the liturgy. It is to commit ourselves to a form of life in which everything we are, everything that we give, is praise:

> You must praise him with the whole of yourselves. Not only must your tongue and your voice praise God, but your conscience must praise him too, and your life and your deeds. What I mean is this: now, while we are gathered in church, we praise God, but when each of you goes off home it looks as though you cease to praise him. But let each one of you not cease to live a good life, and then he or she will be praising God all the time. You only stop praising God when you swerve from just conduct and what pleases him. If you never turn aside from what is right your

tongue is silent, but your life is shouting, and God's ears are attuned to your heart. Just as our ears are sensitive to our voices, so are God's ears sensitive to our thoughts.[2]

It is not just the music of the Mass or the opening hymn or chant that is to be our soundtrack. Praise of God is to become a habit of our hearts. We are to look at our friendships, our family, our jobs—everything—as relationships in which we praise God. Participation in the Mass every week attunes us to a truth that we might have forgotten in the course of our daily lives: that we are called to become a hymn of praise to the world.

> Let the praise of God be in my heart of hearts,
> Let the memory of the Scriptures become my song,
> And let a hymn of love attune me, gracious God,
>   to the peace that you promise to all those who
>   sing a new song to the Lord.

> Alleluia, praise to you O triune God.

QUESTIONS AND PRACTICES

1. What chants or hymns does your parish sing? How do these hymns prepare you to offer praise to God at the beginning of Mass?

2. What distracts you from offering the Mass with full heart and voice? How might you heal yourself of these distractions?

3. In what areas of your life do you need to learn to sing a new song?

CHAPTER FOUR

Reverencing the Altar and Greeting the People

"That I May Come to the Altar of God"

(Ps 43:4)

If you've ever been to an art museum in Europe, you're likely to encounter room after room of panels of the crucified Lord, of his Mother Mary looking with compassion upon the wounded body of her Son, of martyrs in various forms of disfigurement. Because our art museums have saved so many remnants of Catholic culture, we may forget while wandering through these museums that some of these painted panels were originally intended to adorn the altar. These pieces of art were important to the celebration of the Mass.

One of the most spectacular of these is the Isenheim altarpiece, painted by Matthias Grünewald. The Isenheim includes panels depicting Saints Anthony and Paul in the desert, the Annunciation of the Blessed Virgin, the Resurrection and, at the very center of the altarpiece when fully opened, the crucified body of our Lord, Jesus Christ. His arms are twisted upon the cross in a way that no human muscle could move. His body is marked by sores almost too hideous to look upon.

It is important for the viewer of this artwork to know that the Isenheim altarpiece found its home in a hospital where patients were suffering from a terminal plague whose symptoms included the very same sores that marked the body of Christ. When the crucifixion panel of the altar was opened, these patients gazed with wonder upon the Lord of all the earth suffering with them. As Mass was celebrated on the altar, they looked with love upon the suffering Christ, knowing that in the Eucharist they shared in Christ's redemptive suffering upon the cross: "Christ's eternal life, expressed historically in the Resurrection and liturgically in the Eucharist, provided these patients with a model destiny for their own mutilated beings."[3]

THE ALTAR AS PLEDGE OF LOVE

The Isenheim altarpiece helps us understand the strange act of adoration that takes place at the beginning of every Mass. The priest approaches the altar, bowing toward it, kissing it with reverent love, and incensing the cross and the altar together. The word altar should denote to us a place of sacrifice. And the fact that the cross and the altar are incensed together further underline the sacrificial event that takes place at every Mass.

Of course, the altar that is kissed is itself a strange kind of altar. There will be no sacrifice of animals upon the altar stone. Rather, in the Liturgy of the Eucharist, bread and wine will be brought forward. Prayers will be prayed. The memory of Christ's passion and death will be recalled. But no blood (unless something seriously terrible happens) will be spilled upon the altar stone.

The sacrifice of the Mass is Christ's very sacrifice of love. It is the sacrifice of love that is the very origin of the Church to begin with. As Pope Benedict XVI wrote:

> The Church is able to celebrate and adore the mystery of Christ present in the Eucharist precisely because Christ first gave himself to her in the sacrifice of the Cross. The Church's ability to "make" the Eucharist is completely rooted in Christ's self-gift to her. Here we can see more clearly the meaning of Saint John's words: 'he first loved us' (1 Jn 4:19). We, too, at every celebration of the Eucharist, confess the primacy of Christ's gift. The causal influence of the Eucharist at the Church's origins definitively discloses ... the priority of the fact that it was Christ who loved us "first." For all eternity he remains the one who loves us first.[4]

In this sense, our participation in the sacrifice of the Mass is a return gift of love offered to the God who made the first move of love toward us. The God who entered into relationship with us in creation, who called us into covenant in the Exodus, who invited us to love anew in the prophets, who in the fullness of time entered into human history in Jesus Christ: this God made the first move. He loved us first, and he loved us unto the end, dying upon the cross as a supreme act of love. And he still loves us, drawing us closer to his side.

So the priest kisses an altar. Not because Catholics are masochists, having a carnival in the midst of a suffering world. We kiss the altar because it stands among us as a sign of Christ's total act of love. What can we do as human beings but respond with a kiss to such a gift? As the priest kisses the altar, each of us gathered in the sanctuary is to let our whole heart long for the God who first loved us.

BRINGING THE WOUNDS OF THE WORLD TO THE ALTAR

Of course, there is still something very provocative about kissing an altar, that object in the ancient world that functioned as a place of violence and death. Too often American religion serves as a pleasant sedative that enables us to bypass the suffering of the world. Religion is meant to make us feel happy in a world that is sad. To escape the sorrows of the mundane world. You often hear this kind of sentiment in really terrible liturgical music that seems to say: sure, not everything is great, but don't worry, Jesus will make it all better.

Such an approach to religious practice is simply not Catholic. When we go to Mass, we do not leave behind the joys or sorrows that mark us. The Body of Christ throughout the world suffers from the wounds of sin and death, some of which we have inflicted through our own callousness. Psalm 42 cries out to God, "My being thirsts for God, the living God. / When can I go and see the face of God? / My tears have been my food day and night, / as they ask daily, 'Where is your God?'" (Ps 42:3–4).

In the midst of the illness of loved ones we may ask, "Where are you, O God." As we long for a spouse, only to discover relationship after relationship ending, we may cry out, "O God, where are you?" As we suffer through conflict in our marriage, we may cry out, "God, please do something!" As Christians undergo persecution in the Middle East, their voice rings out most clearly: "Act now, my God!"

And yet, the Psalmist does not give up hope: "Bring me to your holy mountain, / to the place of your dwelling, / That I may come to the altar of God, / to God, my joy, my delight" (Ps 43:3–4). To this very altar we bring everything that we have. We bring our joys, which will be offered in love to the Father through the Son. We bring our sorrows, which will also be given as a gift to the triune God. What a radical act to stand before God even when our world is afflicted by violence and sin and death and still hope that God can transform our suffering.

THE REIGN OF PEACE BEGINS

The opening words and actions of the Mass testify to this hope. When we cross ourselves in the name of the Father, and of the Son, and of the Holy Spirit, we demonstrate that God's love has begun to have its reign in our very bodies. It is not simply some ritual tic. It is a continual sign to myself and all the world that my being is already participating in God's very life. I am no longer an individual apart from the rest of the world, apart from God. I exist in the name of the Father, the Son, and the Spirit. Every part of my life is to have meaning in God's sacrificial love.

The priest says to us, "The grace of our Lord Jesus Christ, and the love of God, and the communion of the Holy Spirit be with you all." This is not simply a fancy way for the Church to say "Hello, nice to see you. How have you been?" God's love is already active in assembling us together for this prayer. The Lord is with us, drawing us toward His sacrifice of love upon the altar. At the beginning of Mass, we need only make the space for God to live and move within us. In the Mass, the reign of God's peace, God's love, has begun.

> Take me to your holy altar, O Lord
> And make me a sacrifice of love unto, my God.
> I give to you my joys and sorrows,
> My very self.
> And I receive back from you, a love that makes all
>   things possible.
> Make space within me to receive this love, to be-
>   come this love.
> To share this love to all the ends of the earth.

QUESTIONS AND PRACTICES

1. In kissing the altar, we offer a return gift of love to the God who first loved us. Where have you already noticed God's activity of love in your own life?

2. What joys and sorrows do you want to bring to the altar of God? What do you hope that God will do with your offering?

3. What obstacles in your life exist that make it difficult to accept God's peace in the Mass? What would you need to do in order to move past these obstacles?

4. Buy an icon or other piece of religious art for your home. At the end of every evening, kiss this image. How has the act of kissing this icon or image become a prayer for you?

 CHAPTER FIVE

The Penitential Act

"Lord, Have Mercy"

When I am stuck in traffic, I become a terrible human being. Frustrated, I begin to categorize those around me. The driver who continues to tailgate me becomes the scum of the earth. I imagine said driver, caught by the cops and thrown into jail, receiving the punishment that he deserves for being so inconsiderate. The person driving in front of me, constantly moving from the accelerator to the brake, is the most incompetent person in the world (according to my peerless judgment). I long for an occasion to meet this person one-on-one, letting him know the proper way to drive a car. I blame the bungling management of the city for not creating enough lanes. Everyone receives my wrath. Everyone.

The Church has a name for my peculiar way of passing the time while stuck in traffic: sin. We sin when we imagine ourselves to be the sole character in our story. We sin when we reorder the world according to our own desires, requiring that everyone's wills bend our way. Be more like me, we claim. Think more about me, we say to ourselves. We make ourselves into gods through sin, living no longer as creatures but creators of our own meaning.

Because we are sinners, we stand before God during the introductory rites of the Mass and acknowledge that we often make ourselves into gods rather than worshippers. We acknowledge before God and each other that we are sinners and thus creatures in need of God's grace to perfect us.

SINS OF THE EYES, THE MIND, AND PRIDE OF LIFE

There is something highly counter-cultural in confessing our sins to one another in a public setting. Those of us reared in modern American society are reluctant to even talk about sin. We know that we can do better. We know that we make mistakes. We know that we can try harder to love. But there is an optimism about American culture that makes it difficult for us to say, "There's something wrong with me." That I need help to become who God intended me to be.

I often find this kind of attitude operating among my students. They are unwilling to acknowledge that they need help. I host office hours for four or five hours every week. When students fail, they rarely come to see me without an invitation to do so. They think they might be able to correct all their mistakes on their own. That if they work harder, they'll do better. Sometimes you just need help. Sometimes you can't fix yourself. This is the case with sin. This is the case when our desires become disordered and we worship ourselves rather than God.

The Catholic theological tradition talks about three ways that our desires are disordered, leading to sin. Concupiscence (a word meaning desire or lust) of the flesh is a disordered attraction that we have to material goods.

This kind of sin occurs when find ourselves staring at an attractive person, thinking about them as an object meant to satisfy us. It happens when we go out on a weekend, longing to forget the difficult week that we had on the job by getting as drunk as possible. It is not the possession of the object that is the problem in most cases. Sex can be a good. Drink can be a good. Clothing can be a good. Rather, the problem is the elevation of the material world to a god that we adore.

The second dimension of concupiscence is that of the eyes. This kind of false desire is far more spiritual (and can be more difficult to deal with) than the disordered desires of the flesh. We see someone with a beautiful home and we make a decision that by whatever means necessary we will achieve this good. We purchase clothing or technological gadgets that make us seem beautiful and successful, regardless of the cost. We fall in love with football, bending every aspect of the Sunday Sabbath to watching the NFL. Again, the problem is not with creating a beautiful home, being a successful person, or enjoying leisure. It's that every aspect of our lives must bend to our desires, becoming more central to us than love of God and neighbor. Sin has become so essential to our identities that it occupies our thoughts all day long.

The final dimension of concupiscence is pride of life. Here, sin is at its most radical. I no longer worship a God outside of myself for I have become my own "god." This kind of sin is one that lurks around the corner for every person, especially we Catholics who are actively involved in religious practice. We may see ourselves as religiously complete, no longer in need of God's grace. We may peer upon the rest of humanity, judging our brothers and sisters as the lowest of sinners (while seeing ourselves as the height of sanctity). Pride of life is the sin that constantly tempts us. To free ourselves from it requires God's persistent gift of love.

THE PENITENTIAL ACT AS MEDICINE FOR DISORDERED DESIRE

While there are various options for the penitential rite, each of them intends to heal us of our disordered desire. We stand before God and admit that we have adored at altars of our own creation: of food and drink, of ambition and consumption, of a love of self that is forgetful of the other. We pray together:

> I confess to almighty God
> and to you, my brothers and sisters,
> that I have greatly sinned,
> in my thoughts and in my words,
> in what I have done and in what I have failed to do,
> through my fault, through my fault,
> through my most grievous fault;
> therefore I ask blessed Mary ever-Virgin
> all the Angels and Saints,
> and you, my brothers and sisters,
> to pray for me to the Lord our God.

This prayer, the *Confiteor*, is not about self-hatred. It is instead an act of praise in which I acknowledge before God that I am not the creator of the world. I have sinned. I have said hateful words against a coworker, against a spouse, against a child. I have grown addicted to staring at images of half-naked men or women, treating the human body as a piece of meat for me to consume. I have failed to enter into relationship with the poor, with the suffering, with all those on the margins of our society. I avoid prayer because I am too busy, quickly turning my work and my family life into an idol. I have chosen to do this. Me. Not because I was poorly parented or because my friends are insufferable or because no one supports me at work. I have sinned: *My fault, my fault, my most grievous fault.*

It is only through this disposition of acknowledging our faults that God can act. In Catholicism, when we confess our sins, we are not dwelling on our misery. Rather we are already praising the God who always forgives us, the God who seeks to pour out a new supply of grace to heal our wounds of sin. In the Penitential Act at every Mass, we anticipate singing out: *Glory to God in the highest, and on earth peace to people of good will.*

A CULTURAL AND COSMIC RESTORATION

Because at every Mass we acknowledge our identity as one sinner among many within the community of faith, we come to terms with the fact that we all have sinned, harming the Body of Christ and thus the human family. For the Catholic, there is no such thing as private sin. Our individual disordered desires have created cultures oriented around a lust for domination. As Pope Francis writes in *Laudato Si'*:

> When we fail to acknowledge as part of reality the worth of a poor person, a human embryo, a person with disabilities—to offer just a few examples—it becomes difficult to hear the cry of nature itself; everything is

connected. Once the human being declares independence from reality and behaves with absolute dominion, the very foundations of our life begin to crumble, for "instead of carrying out his role as a cooperator with God in the work of creation, man sets himself up in place of God and thus ends up provoking a rebellion on the part of nature."[5]

Every sin that we commit harms each one of us. Catholics must not support abortion. But we may find ourselves judging unwed mothers, making it difficult for these women to choose to carry the child to term. We might not pollute entire rivers. But we may foster in our children habits of productivity that are harmful to the world. We might not force the immigrant to cross a desert without food, clothing, or water. But we may have grown cold to the plight of those on the margins, happy to live our lives isolated from those who hunger and thirst for food and drink. For love itself.

All of this is not to make us feel bad about ourselves. Rather, it is to recognize that sin has a real effect on the world and our relationships with one another. Accordingly, to confess our sins before God and one another, to ask for the prayers of the saints, to pledge to live a life of worship rather than self-adoration—this is the first step of our healing. It is the first step in acknowledging that we are creatures and not God. In this acknowledgment, we already begin the praise that will restore creation to its vocation of praise.

Lord, have mercy on me, who fails to love those on the margins of our world.

Lord, have mercy on me, who prays so little and
worries so much.

Lord, have mercy on me, who spends so much
time in front of the TV, who cannot take his
eyes away from his smartphone to say one kind
word to his child.

Lord, have mercy on me, who has become so at-
tached to being right, to being the best, to
achieving success at all costs.

Lord, have mercy on me, a sinner.

Lord, have mercy on us sinners.

QUESTIONS AND PRACTICES

1. Where do you notice patterns of sin in your life? What
   disordered desires do you see at the heart of these patterns of sin?

2. What practices might you take up to move away from
   these sins?

3. How has your understanding of sin changed by acknowledging, as we do in the *Confiteor*, that each of us is
   responsible for the sins of the world?

4. Before bed every evening, do an examination of con-
   science in which you acknowledge where you loved God
   well and where you didn't. Bring these sins to mind before the beginning of every Mass.

CHAPTER SIX

Gloria in Excelsis
"You Alone Are the Holy One"

Over the course of a football season, the Notre Dame Glee Club sings the fight song of all of Notre Dame's opponents before every football game on campus. In my four years in this (to my judgment, esteemed) group, I realized that the fight song genre necessitates repeating yourself many times, together with presuming a proper sense of your team's own self-importance. The Washington State Cougars are exhorted more than once to "Fight, Fight, Fight." The University of Michigan football team is hailed as valiant victors, while also being praised as the best in the West (I suppose there may be some geographic challenges to such a claim). The crowd cheering on the Fighting Irish of Notre Dame are told to "wake up the echoes," whatever the odds may be.

Fight songs are repeated until they become part of the collective memory of the stadium, bringing everyone together in praise of the team. In some ways, the singer is joining not simply with everyone in the stadium but every fan across the ages who has praised the beloved alma mater.

There are, of course, problems with the union that fight songs promote. Implicitly, the song is sung not simply as a way of joining the stadium together. The fight song draws a line in the sand: will you belong to us, the home team, or will you root for the Trojans of Southern California? There is a militancy to the fight song that is nearly unavoidable. Not everyone can belong because there are those who are not with us, the home team.

The hymn of praise—*Glory to God in the highest, and on earth peace to people of good will*—is the fight song of the angels and saints, the Church militant and victorious, in which no one is excluded from the peace of God's reign. As we sing this hymn of praise each week in Mass (except during Advent and Lent), we join our voices not simply with one another. We are united together with all those who worship the God of hosts whether gathered in our tiny parish church or enjoying the beatific vision of God. This is the fight song of those who have chosen the way of peace.

THE INCARNATION AND THE MASS

The *Gloria*, like many hymns and prayers of the Mass, includes various parts. The first part of the *Gloria* (quoted above) is a citation from the nativity of Jesus in the Gospel of Luke. The full text states:

> Now there were shepherds in that region living in the fields and keeping the night watch over their flock. The angel of the Lord appeared to them and the glory of the Lord shone around them, and they were struck with great fear. The angel said to them, "Do not be afraid; for behold, I proclaim to you good news of great joy that will be for all the

people. For today in the city of David a savior
has been born for you who is Messiah and
Lord. And this will be a sign for you: you will
find an infant wrapped in swaddling clothes
and lying in a manger." And suddenly there
was a multitude of the heavenly host with the
angel, praising God and saying:

"Glory to God in the highest
and on earth peace to those on whom his favor
  rests." (Lk 2:8–14)

This encounter between the angels and the shepherds is important for understanding the spiritual meaning of singing the *Gloria*. Shepherds within Israel are not
simply, as it is often presented, meager farmhands. After
all, David, the great king of Israel, comes from a line of
shepherds. Thus, although the encounter between the
angels and shepherds may happen in the midst of night,
hidden from the sight of the rest of the world, there is a
political implication to the encounter. The angels, by ap-
pearing to shepherds, are announcing the beginning of
God's reign of peace. The shepherd kings of Israel have
come to greet the newborn king of the world, born in the
silence of the night.

This interpretation of the encounter is underlined
throughout the text. "Good news," or *gospel*, is often used
in Greco-Roman literature to denote a military victory.
Christ has appeared in the city of David, Bethlehem, the
great king's city. This remarkable victory, rather than a
matter of military prowess, is being carried out through
the poverty of an infant in swaddling clothes, lying in
the feed trough of animals. This seemingly impoverished

victory is praised by the angels who proclaim that the glory of God now dwells among mortals, beginning the reign of peace.

The first two lines of the *Gloria* are in fact essential to understanding what takes place at Mass. In this small parish church, where the lives of men and women unfold over the years, the Word still becomes flesh. God's glory appears in the reading of Scripture, in the body of Christ assembled, in the priest's ministry, and most of all in the Eucharistic species. To most, the remarkable vision of what is happening cannot be seen. God's glory is still unfolding in a hidden way, in the lives of those who assemble to offer divine praise. Here, in this parish church, the reign of God's peace announced by the angels continues for the benefit of all the world.

This is proclaimed to us at the beginning of Mass. And we join in the song of the angels, letting our voice enter into the heavenly chorus. Heaven's peace becomes the earth's when we sing this song, making it our own in our hearts.

REPETITION AND PRAISE

The second part of the *Gloria* moves from salvation history into a contemplation of God's very being as Trinity. The text states: We praise you, we bless you, we adore you, we glorify you, we give you thanks for your great glory. To an English speaker, this seems highly repetitive. What's the difference between praise, blessing, adoration, glorification, and thanksgiving? Is the Church just being inefficient?

In fact, the Catholic Mass, growing out of Scriptural poetry, has always repeated itself. We repeat ourselves because no word that we utter is sufficient to praise God. We repeat ourselves because every word we say enables us to ascend closer to God, to lift up our hearts in praise of God's love. We repeat ourselves because God never tires of hearing our simple speech offered as a gift, akin to the way that parents delight in the earliest stages of a child's speech.

And our song continues to praise the triune God revealed by Jesus Christ. The *Gloria* is a Trinitarian hymn in which we praise the Father, the Son, and the Holy Spirit. At the central axis of the hymn is Jesus, the Word made flesh, who reveals to us the splendor and mercy of God's reign on earth. He is the reason we are gathered together for prayer this day. It is because of his mercy that our voices can sound out in song, joining the festive chorus of the angelic host.

The Church sings this song. And every time our voices enter into this praise, the glory of God revealed through Jesus Christ becomes present to us once again:

> Every day that the Church lives, every time the Church gathers her children in prayer, and particularly when she assembles them for the Eucharist, a new light flashes across the world and the Church beholds, with mingled joy and longing, the approach of the Kingdom of God, the advent, in spite of every obstacle, of the consummation of the great plan: that glory will come to God, and to men of God's choice, peace and salvation.[6]

Singing the *Gloria* is not an option for the Church. In the Archdiocese of Boston, where I lived for years, too many of the parishes recited this text so as to save time at Mass. In failing to sing this hymn of praise every Sunday that it is permitted, at every feast, we fail to let the angelic song ring out through the ages. We fail to let God's glory be known in the world.

If the *Gloria* is the fight song of the Church, then we need to sing it, letting it echo in every village, town, and city in the world. And through this peaceful hymn of praise, perhaps God's reign of peace will extend even farther. From that little hamlet of Bethlehem to the hill of Calvary to the empty tomb, and even now to my home where God's peace should reign supreme: Glory to God in the highest, and on earth peace to people of good will.

> You created us in your image and likeness, *let all the world praise you.*
>
> You called us into covenant, sharing your life with us, *let all the world praise you.*
>
> You never neglected us in our sins, bringing us back again and again to new life, *let all the world praise you.*
>
> You revealed your glorious presence to hidden shepherds, *let all the world praise you.*
>
> You still bring forth your peace to the world at every Mass where we sing your praises, *let all the world praise you.*
>
> May my life become to the world the peaceful song of God's love, *let all the world praise you.*

QUESTIONS AND PRACTICES

1. Compose your own hymn of praise to God for all that he has done for you, using images or words from the Scriptures. What have you learned about God's glory?

2. The Church, in her celebration of Mass, is to become a song of peace for the world. How can your parish show forth to the world the peace of God?

CHAPTER SEVEN

The Collect

"Let Us Pray"

When I speak to undergraduates who are bored by Mass, they often note how formal the prayers seem. Isn't it easier to just speak to God on your own? Why do we have to use the words of the Church to share our thoughts with God? I would be more interested in going to Mass if I could speak to God using my own experience, my own words.

In some ways, my undergraduates are right. We do need to speak to God out of our heartfelt desires to commune with the Father, the Son, and the Holy Spirit. Every moment of our days should be an offering to God such that when we go the gym, when we head to work, when we eat lunch, when we drive home, and when we go to sleep, our thoughts are always dedicated to praise of God. Speaking to God in our own words, in our heart, often facilitates a personal encounter with Jesus the Bridegroom, the Lord, the Good Shepherd who loves us unto the end.

But learning to speak to God well requires learning a vocabulary and a grammar. Is Shakespeare's love poetry less beautiful, less heartfelt because it takes the form of a sonnet? Of course not. Otherwise, why would generation after generation return to these sonnets, discovering there once again a language to speak about love? Does the music of Taylor Swift misrepresent young love because she writes songs that rhyme? No, the rhythm of the song is what captures our attention to begin with.

In the opening prayer or collect of every Mass, we encounter a prayer style that has a definitive form. If we learn to pay attention to these prayers, contemplating the images that are present in these collects, then we will learn over the course of a lifetime to speak to God through the voice of the Church herself. Our capacity for prayer, for encountering the living God through human speech, will increase.

THE STRUCTURE OF A COLLECT PRAYER

A collect prayer receives its name because it "collects" the prayers of the assembly gathered for worship. After the *Gloria*, a moment of silence should fill the church. Here, the entire assembly should be praying to God within their hearts. After a few moments, the priest joins his hands together and invites us to pray. Now this is not the first time that we have been praying during Mass. Rather, the individual prayers that have been welling up in our hearts are now joined together through the voice of the Church.

This opening collect is a prayer that typically changes every week during the liturgical year. These prayers, taken from the history of the Church's liturgy, are filled with images that invite us to contemplate what God has accomplished through his Son, Jesus Christ.

A collect prayer has a definite structure, arising out of Jewish prayer traditions. Fr. Michael Lang describes this structure as:

1. An address to God, generally to the Father
2. A relative or participial clause referring to some attribute of God or to one of his saving acts
3. The petition, either in the imperative or in the subjunctive
4. The reason or desired result for which the petition is made
5. The conclusion[7]

A sample collect prayer can help us make sense of this structure. On Holy Thursday, the opening collect states:

> O God, who have called us to participate
> in this most sacred Supper,
> in which your Only Begotten Son,
> when about to hand himself over to death,
> entrusted to the Church a sacrifice new for all
>   eternity,
> the banquet of his love,
> grant, we pray,
> that we may draw from so great a mystery,
> the fullness of charity and of life.
> Through our Lord Jesus Christ, your Son,
> who lives and reigns with you in the unity of the
>   Holy Spirit,
> one God, for ever and ever.

The prayer is addressed to God, using the Latin word *Deus*. While typically we refer to God in general, the collect prayers of the Church, with a couple of exceptions, are addressed to the Father through the Son in the unity of the Holy Spirit. The collect prayer is a Trinitarian prayer, as we see in the closing lines above.

The relative clause of this collect prayer recalls Christ's own invitation for the Church to participate in the Last Supper: "who have called us to participate in this most sacred Supper, in which your only begotten Son, when about to hand himself over to death, entrusted to the Church a sacrifice new for all eternity, the banquet of his love." There is a paradox in the imagery here. The "Only Begotten Son," who is light from light, God from God, the eternal God who exists outside of space and time, celebrates a meal at the precise moment in which he hands himself over as a sacrifice of love for humanity. God has entered into our history.

Yet this historical event is not to remain in the past. From the mystery of this Last Supper, we ask God to draw us (*hauriámus*) into the fullness of divine love and life revealed in Jesus' death and resurrection: "grant, we pray, that we may draw from so great a mystery, the fullness of charity and of life." The Latin word *hauriámus* also has the connotation of drinking from a cup or spilling blood unto death. In this sense, we are asking God that the whole Church may become better disciples of Jesus, learning to love unto the end like our Savior. We are to imitate Christ's death in our lives so that new life can be brought to the world. And our ability to participate in this death and resurrection actually takes place at Mass.

As noted, the prayer concludes with a doxology in which we pray through Jesus Christ who remains alive and active among us as the resurrected Lord. We trust that our prayer will be listened to by the Father—that our requests will be heard—because of the Spirit "inspiring" our prayer. We're not just addressing God on our own terms here. In the Church's prayer, it is God who is making it possible for us to pray at all.

REFRESHING HOPE

While this is the structure of the collect prayer, one may ask why this really matters for those of us trying to celebrate the Mass today. The question still remains: is there not an easier way to pray?

In fact, the form of the collect prayer reveals something about what we hope for at every Mass. God has acted in the past. This narrative of God's love is revealed in the Scriptures and in the lives of the saints. But what do these events have to do with me here and now?

The collect prayer, as a structure, dares to hope that the way God has acted in the past will inform his action within the present. Through remembering what God has done from age to age, we are slowly formed to recognize where God is acting in our own lives at present. Two examples will suffice to show us how these prayers form us to hope anew.

On the feast of Christmas, at Mass during the day, the Church prays:

> O God, who wonderfully created the dignity of
> human nature
> and still more wonderfully restored it,
> grant, we pray,
> that we may share in the divinity of Christ,
> who humbled himself to share in our humanity.

Who lives and reigns with you in the unity of the
Holy Spirit,
one God, for ever and ever.

In this collect prayer, the Church is reminded that the feast of Christmas is not just a quaint celebration of Jesus' birthday. Instead, the God who created human beings out of nothing has now restored humanity to what we were intended to be. As the Word becomes flesh, sharing fully in what it means to be human, we are invited to enter into the divine life of the Son. We share in this divinity not by seizing power, by grasping control, but by emptying ourselves in humble love. Christmas isn't just one day. It's the feast of a form of life in which we learn to become like God through the art of self-giving love. Every time we come to the Supper of the Lamb, we are invited to share in the humility of Jesus, eating his Body and drinking his Blood. The Nativity of the Lord, Christmas, still has an effect here and now.

The sacrament of marriage also has a collect prayer, one that all married couples should reflect on:

O God, who consecrated the bond of Marriage
by so great a mystery
that in the wedding covenant you foreshadow
the Sacrament of Christ and his Church,
grant, we pray, to these your servants,
that what they receive in faith
they may live out in deeds.
Through our Lord Jesus Christ, your Son,
who lives and reigns with you in the unity of the
Holy Spirit,
one God, for ever and ever.

This collect prayer, drawing from St. Paul's account of marriage as a mystery, or sacrament, signifying the union of Christ and the Church, calls the entire Church to remember what is taking place in the sacrament of marriage. This is no mere civil union. Instead, it is a sacrament in which the union of husband and wife represents to all the world the love of Christ and the Church. The couple marrying this day are prayed for by the voice of the whole Church. We pray that the mystery that unfolds in the marriage rite, the consecration of this couple into a sign of Christ's self-giving love, may in fact become the form of life that the couple chooses. Every married couple in the assembly is "renewed" in their vows by hearing this prayer and by recommitting themselves to Christ's love for each other and therefore for the world.

NOURISHING OUR IMAGINATIONS

The collect prayer, while it may seem formal, is actually a nourishment for our imaginations. We hear what God has accomplished through Christ. We contemplate the wonders of salvation through images handed on to us from the early and medieval Church. And we trust that what the triune God has accomplished in love is still unfolding even now within the Church. By praying the collect prayer not simply in Church but at home, we are formed so that we can see God's presence and become the disciple that God has intended us to be.

> O almighty Father,
> through the sweet speech of your Church,
> you have formed us to offer praises and prayers to
>   you.

> Teach your Church to marvel at the gift of your
>   Son for the world
> and give us faith, hope, and love so that we may
>   become this gift for others.
> Through our Lord Jesus Christ,
> who lives and reigns with you in the unity of the
>   Holy Spirit,
> one God for ever and ever.
> Amen.

QUESTIONS AND PRACTICES

1. Write your own collect prayer for an upcoming feast. Use as many images from Scripture or phrases from the liturgy as you can.

2. How do you see what God has accomplished in Christ unfolding in your own life right now?

3. What would it cost to live out the kind of discipleship asked for by the collect for the Feast of the Nativity, above? For the collect of the sacrament of marriage?

4. Read the collect prayer the week before Mass. Pray it every morning and ask God for some particular need or grace in your life out of the prayer.

 CHAPTER EIGHT

The Word and Silence

"My Word ... Shall Not Return to Me Void"

(Is 55:11)

We were waiting. For two hours we sat at the hospital, staring at a television on which absurd adolescent cartoons without recognizable plot unfolded before our glassy eyes. Our son, whom we were adopting, had been delivered two hours before through C-section. An hour or so after the surgery, a nurse came to us to say that there had been problems during delivery. Our son could not immediately breathe and was being taken to the NICU. The longer the silence, the greater our fear.

At the end of the two-hour wait, we were called into the NICU and given hospital gowns to wear over our street clothes and instructions on how to wash our hands. As we entered our son's room and met the tiny creature, his chest expanded in and out at what seemed like an un-sustainable pace. At seven and a half pounds, he was a sight to behold.

We spent that first evening of our son's life at his bedside. My wife and I rarely exchanged words, keeping a holy silence before the fragile life for which we were now responsible. That delicate person whom we already loved. The night moved along as nurse after nurse entered the room, as alarms from machines sent us into a panic each time they interrupted our silent vigil.

And finally, as day broke, word came from the doctor that our son was starting to breathe on his own. The silence of expectation, of fear and hope alike, had been pierced by the power of a word: "He is going to be okay." From our previously sealed lips poured forth words of gratitude. We looked at our son, held his hand, and from our lips came the name of our beloved child, "Tommy, it's going to be okay."

SILENCE AND THE WORD

We are not the first human beings to experience the power of silence interrupted by a word. Lovers know what it is like to await those three words that always come as gift: "I love you." We have experienced the silent response that is appropriate before the beauty of the created order in which our lack of speech is an act of praise offered as a return gift to the magnificent Creator. We have stood vigil beside the bed of a relative, praying in sorrow as death descends upon our mother, our father, even our child. Silence is necessary for the one who worships the God who speaks in silence and word alike.

And the Scriptures clearly describe God as speaking both through silence and speech. In the Book of Genesis, before God creates the world, there is the silence of nothing. In the midst of this formless void, God speaks a creative word, breaking through the silence of nothing, giving life to all the world. The Psalmist cries out to God, asking to hear his consoling speech in the midst of total abandonment: "My God, I call by day, but you do not answer; / by night, but I have no relief" (Ps 22:3). Never giving up hope, this same Psalmist (whose words are spoken by Christ upon the cross) awaits God's living word, "For God has not spurned or disdained / the misery of this poor wretch / ... but heard me when I cried out" (Ps 22:25). God will speak from the silence, and when he does, this word will renew the world: "So shall my word be / that goes forth from my mouth; / It shall not return to me void, / but shall do my will, / achieving the end for which I sent it" (Is 55:11).

THE LITURGY OF THE WORD

At the beginning of the Liturgy of the Word, we sit down in silent expectation for God's living word to speak once again. In the silence of our church, the word will echo forth to re-create our very hearts. The words of Scripture will console us. They will challenge us. They will bring us once again into the memory of the Church, creating in us a desire for God to act again in our midst.

But, our parishes are so uncomfortable with silence. Perhaps it is the modern problem *par excellence*. We wake up from the silence of sleep and immediately experience the noise of email, of social media, of televisions noisily proclaiming the end of this political party or that one. We get into cars where we are inundated with the idle chatter of morning radio. At the office, the noise continues as we receive email after email, phone call after phone call. We rush home to take our children to various activities, all the while talking on the cell phone to the spouse we haven't really spent time with in days. We stare at the television at the conclusion of the day, getting lost in more speech. We go to bed, happy to have some experience of silence wash over us.

So it's not a surprise that too many of our parishes do not adequately wait with silent expectation for God to speak in the Liturgy of the Word. The lectors move quickly from reading to reading. Priests want the Mass to move along, to keep the entire liturgy around an hour or so. We have grown uncomfortable with the silence. Afraid that if we paused for a moment God might really speak to us through the Scriptures that we read together.

CREATING SILENCE

As lay people, we cannot usually control the amount of silence that occurs at Mass, but we can form ourselves in an interior silence as a way of preparing to hear God's voice. As Thomas Merton writes:

> There should be at least a room, or some corner where no one will find you and disturb you or notice you. You should be able to untether yourself from the world and set yourself free, loosing all the fine strings and strands of tension that bind you, by sight, by sound, by thought, to the presence of other men.[8]

Through the Scriptures read at Mass, God is not simply speaking to the Church in general but to each of the desires that occupy our minds and thoughts. In order to really participate in the Mass, we need to become lovers of silence, practiced in hearing God's voice working in our lives every day. Before Mass, we should read the Scriptures of the day and spend fifteen minutes with God, listening to the creative word that the Incarnate Word offers us. God is always speaking, but are we listening?

In addition to an encounter with Scripture in one's own home, it's important to spend time in silence in the quiet sanctuary of the church. Our parishes have become spaces of constant devotion and activity. Before Mass, parishioners gather to pray the Rosary and the novena of the day together. We practice the music of the day, otherwise who would be able to sing the *Sanctus*? (Generally, everyone has heard one of the five Mass settings done in most parishes.) Before and after Mass, conversations fill the space, since these help form Christian community. In each of these ways, we create parish churches where noise is more expected than silence. Where our speech becomes more important than God's. And we destroy the remarkable gift that parish churches can offer to the modern person who is longing for a moment alone before God.

Again, turning to Merton:

> Let there always be quiet, dark churches in which men can take refuge. Places where they can kneel in silence. Houses of God, filled with His silent presence. There, even when they do not know how to pray, at least they can be still and breathe easily. Let there be a place somewhere in which you can breathe naturally, quietly, and not have to take your breath in continuous short gasps. A place where your mind can be idle, forget its concerns, descend into silence, and worship the Father in secret.

There can be no contemplation where there is no secret.[9]

In order for us to hear God's word, to grow accustomed to delighting in the salvation of divine speech, we must become practiced in the art of silence. The Mass is not about communicating our speech. Our words. Our ideas. But creating a space in our lives where we can encounter the creative, life-giving word of God.

> Give me the grace, O gracious God, to sit in
>   silence before your living word.
> Create in me a heart attentive to your whispered
>   wisdom.
> Make our parishes sanctuaries of silent devotion,
>   where we meet face-to-face the God who fills
>   the world with his loving word.
> Harbor in my heart the soothing silence of your
>   love.

QUESTIONS AND PRACTICES

1. For the next week, spend fifteen minutes reading the Scriptures for the Mass of the day and sitting in silence. What is God saying to you in the midst of the silence?

2. How might your parish create more opportunities for silence at Mass?

3. What in your life is keeping you away from being silent before God? How could you decrease the amount of noise in your life?

CHAPTER NINE

The Liturgy of the Word

"When I Found Your Words, I Devoured Them"

(Jer 15:16)

When Americans read the Bible, they tend to read it as a source for broad moral guidelines about how to live a pretty good life. Having trouble with your marriage? Turn to this passage. Don't know what you're doing with your life? That's fine, in Scripture you'll discover what God hopes for you. Want to figure out the right political solution to some of the problems that we're going through in the United States? It's in the Good Book.

This approach, while certainly respectful of the Bible's authority, is not how Catholics read Scripture. To fruitfully participate in the Liturgy of the Word, we have to know something about how the Church reads the Bible, especially at Mass. We are not individuals simply encountering a text that will provide moral guidelines for our life. We are not isolated persons coming to a private interpretation of what the Bible means for me. Instead, in the Scriptures we are encountering the history of God's salvation for human beings. It is a history that allows us to make sense of the world around us.

WHAT IS A LECTIONARY?

If you've ever served as a lector at Mass, you know that the Church uses a collection of the Scriptures called a Lectionary. In the history of Christianity, there have been a number of different ways to divide the Bible over the course of the year. At the Second Vatican Council, the Catholic Church revised its lectionary to include more readings from the Old Testament, in addition to adopting a Sunday cycle of readings in which the Mass-goer would hear much of the Bible over a three-year period.

The Sunday Lectionary includes four different texts from Scripture every week. The first reading is taken from the Old Testament (except during the season of Easter in which we hear from The Acts of the Apostles). This reading is meant to relate to the Gospel of the day. The next scriptural reading is the psalm of the day, which is to be sung. The second reading is generally a New Testament letter read semicontinuously. Except for rare circumstances, it is thematically unrelated to either the Old Testament or the Gospel.

Lastly, there is the Gospel itself. In Year A, we read from the Gospel of Matthew. In Year B, we read from the Gospel of Mark as well as the sixth chapter of the Gospel of John. In Year C, we read the Gospel of Luke. And throughout the year, we also hear from the Gospel of John, especially during the season of Easter.

It is important to know the mechanics of the lectionary, but if we want to understand the story that the Church tells over the course of the year in the Mass, it is even more important to understand the plot of the story itself. Every story needs an interpreter, someone who can guide the loose threads together into a coherent narrative. We have all known people who are unable to tell a coherent story. They include unnecessary details and leave their listeners lost, unable to make sense of how the parts of the story are connected.

In the case of the Liturgy of the Word, we are hearing a coherent story about God's immense love for humanity. The Scriptures, as the Church reads them at Mass, are not simply full of moral aphorisms or instructions for living a decent life. Instead, they are an encounter with God's slow process of bringing all human beings toward their final end: the transformation of women and men into a work of love.

Every aspect of Scripture, for a Catholic, is oriented toward an encounter with Jesus Christ, who is the Word made flesh. He is the one who reveals to us that God is love itself. And if we love the God that Jesus reveals to us, meaning that we love our neighbor as our very selves, then we enter into union with this God.

THE GOLDEN THREAD OF SCRIPTURE

How does one see this single thread running throughout the entire Bible? To grasp at this thread, we have to get over an assumption that is prevalent among many—that there is something called an Old Testament God and a New Testament God. The former God is judgmental, prone to fits of violence, and overly concerned about the Law. The supposed God of the New Testament is really concerned about love. He has no interest in the Law. And he wants everyone to be super nice to one another, which is really the heart of religion to begin with. This false way of reading Scripture is present in the early Church, in American history, and of course today. When teaching Scripture to my undergraduates, it's the very first assumption that I must dispose of.

If this is the wrong way to read the Bible, how do we find the right thread? Pope Emeritus Benedict XVI suggests such a thread in his document *Verbum Domini* ("The Word of the Lord"):

> It is very beautiful to see how the entire Old Testament ... appears to us as a history in which God communicates his word: indeed, "by his covenant with Abraham (cf. Gen 15:18) and, through Moses, with the race of Israel (cf. Ex 24:8), he gained a people for himself, and to them he revealed himself in words and deeds as the one, living, and true God.
>
> It was his plan that Israel might learn by experience God's ways with humanity and, by listening to the voice of God speaking to them through prophets, might gradually understand his ways more fully and more clearly, and make them more widely known about the nations....
>
> This "condescension" of God is accomplished surpassingly in the incarnation of the Word. The eternal Word, expressed in creation and communicated in salvation history, in Christ became a man, "born of woman" (Gal 4:4). Here the word finds expression not primarily in discourse, concepts, or rules. Here we are set before the

very person of Jesus. His unique and singu-
lar history is the definitive word which God
speaks to humanity.[10]

The thread of the Scriptures is the story of a God
who has become involved in human history. It is the God
who has created the world from nothing, as an act of love.
The God who invites Adam and Eve to share in God's
very life in paradise. The God who responds to the fall of
Adam and Eve not with vengeance but with the wounded
heart of a lover, who woos sinful humanity back to relationship. The God who promises fidelity to Abraham, to
Isaac, and to Jacob, and who lives out this covenant promise with Moses. The God who gives the Law on Mt. Sinai,
offering a tender curriculum of love if Israel chooses to
follow it. The God who forgives with mercy Israel again
and again, even when they forget to love the orphan and
the widow, when they worship foreign gods. The God
who enters into exile with Israel, sharing in their suffering, inviting them back to a new Temple where worship
and thus God's presence is once again available.

It is the story of the God who in the fullness of time
entered into human history as one of us, loving us even
unto death. The God who still dwells with us through the
Holy Spirit, leading us to encounter again the Word made
flesh, Jesus Christ. The God who is still available to us
through the life of the Church, Christ's very Body in the
world. The God who will one day take up all of creation
into heaven itself, where there will be no enemies, no
wars, no tears. Only praise of God. This is the story that
we hear every year in the Lectionary, the story that helps
us make sense of life itself.

THIS IS MY STORY

We listen to this story every year because it is the one that makes sense of every other story. There are lots of stories out there about the world. There are stories that tell us that profit and prestige are the way to a happy life. There are stories that reduce our beauty to our sex appeal. There are stories that say that the unborn child, the immigrant, and the prisoner are expendable human beings. These are lies, bad stories caused by human sin.

There are also the stories of our lives. God, as has already been said, isn't just the God who enters into our lives once upon a time. God is active here and now. Through reading the Bible, we come to see how my story is actually being shaped by the story of salvation told in the Church.

The Scriptures are the true story that we savor year after year, enabling us to read our stories anew. Like the prophet Jeremiah, we are to listen to this story and rejoice in what we hear: "When I found your words, I devoured them; / they became my joy and the happiness of my heart" (Jer 15:16). The Liturgy of the Word is an occasion to listen to God's love story for humanity. A love story that did not end with the Resurrection and Ascension but is continuing even now in my little town, in my big city, in every nook and cranny of the world in which the story is told. The heart full of gratitude we have in hearing this story is the one that we bring every Sunday to the altar. It is this heart of gratitude caused by an encounter with God's revelation of love that will change the world.

> God, who first loved the human race,
> creating us in your image and likeness

and renewing us through our Lord Jesus;
Assist your Church in contemplating this love
    story
with all the saints in heaven
so that we may become for the world
the image and likeness of God's love
for all those we encounter.
We ask this through Christ our Lord. Amen.

QUESTIONS AND PRACTICES

1. What are your favorite stories from the Bible? What do these stories reveal to you about God's love for the human race?

2. How has listening to Scripture year after year led you to a deeper understanding of who God is?

3. Before going to Mass one Sunday, read the Scriptures. Try to determine the link between the Old Testament reading and the Gospel. How is this link related to the golden thread above? If you can't figure it out, ask a priest or catechist in your parish.

CHAPTER TEN

Responsorial Psalm

"How Long Must I Carry Sorrow in My Soul"
(Ps 13:3)

No priest or deacon I know preaches on the psalms. It's almost as if, at every Mass, the purpose of the sung psalm for the day is simply to provide a nice break from listening to a lector. As if the Church says to herself, "Wow, that was a lot of listening. It would be good now to sing something in order to take a break from the strenuous three to five minutes of attention to the Scriptures that we just carried out." While preachers would never say that they believe the psalm is a mere musical interlude, they are saying exactly this by ignoring it in the homily.

In reality, the singing of a psalm after the first reading reveals something important about the entire Mass. In the psalms, we encounter and become, through the Spirit, Christ's very voice offered to the Father in love. Every human affection, every desire, is brought before God upon the altar. We hear God's loving word, and we respond in a song of gratitude, of praise, of lament, and of joy. Through the psalm, we anticipate the Eucharist where we offer a return gift of love to the God who has revealed himself in the sacrificial love of the Son.

PSALMODY AS THE SPEECH OF CHRIST'S BODY

Readers of this book of the Bible know that the Psalmist offers to God every human emotion that is possible. He complains to God, "How many are my foes, LORD! How many rise against me!" (Ps 3:2). In the midst of this turmoil, he nonetheless trusts in the God of Abraham, Isaac, and Jacob: "LORD my God, in you I take refuge; rescue me; save me from all who pursue me" (Ps 7:2). The Psalmist confesses to God his own sinfulness: "For I know my offense; my sin is always before me. Against you alone have I sinned; I have done such evil in your sight" (Ps 51:5–6). He cries out to God in total abandonment, as he sings a song in exile on the rivers of Babylon (cf. Ps 137). And often, he breaks out in praise for all that God has done: "Let everything that has breath / give praise to the LORD! / Hallelujah!" (Ps 150:6).

When the early Church inherited the Book of Psalms, they recognized the diversity of affections that are present in this book of the Bible. Yet more importantly, they knew that these very psalms were the ones that Jesus himself used in prayer before the Father. Because Jesus is resurrected from the dead, ascended into heaven, and alive as head of the Church, the singer of the psalms is not simply the individual Christian but Christ himself. As Augustine preaches, "And you will remember, beloved, whose voice we are accustomed to hear in all the psalms: the voice of one who comprises both head and body. The head is in heaven, the body on earth, but where the head has gone the body is to follow."[11]

In this sense, when we sing the psalms, it is never our voice alone that is praying. Rather, Christ is taking up everything that it means to be human in the Church. When we express to the Father our sorrows in the world, Christ sings this hymn for us as the Son of the Father. When we praise God, it is Christ singing God's goodness for us. The psalms enact the divine-human exchange that takes place in the Incarnation. Our humanity, expressed in the affections of the Psalmist, is taken up before God and offered to the Father. Jesus, as our friend, the one who knows us best of all, prays in and with us.

This is important for participation in the Mass. Many times, we come to the Eucharist and we don't have the voice to pray. When my wife and I were struggling with infertility, I often could not pray at Mass. I was so angry with the God who seemed to ignore my prayers. Yet in the psalms I was given a language to speak to God. I could join my voice with the Church's voice and cry out, "How long must I carry sorrow in my soul, / grief in my heart day after day? / How long will my enemy triumph over me?" (Ps 13:3).

Even more comforting than having this prayer to offer to God, I knew that I was not praying alone. Jesus, the Word made flesh, my brother, was praying these very words for me. My voice, my shaking voice of sorrow, became Christ's voice. My sorrow, in the process of singing the psalms, became an offering to the Father.

WORDS MATTER

Because the words of the psalms are so important, the music that we use in praying them should not overpower our attention to the text. I have often attended LifeTeen

Masses where a drum and a saxophone are played as the cantor sings the psalm. The text is overpowered by instrumentation—you can barely hear the words that the cantor sings.

Likewise, there are many settings of the psalms in the Church that fail to grasp the link between the words and the affections that the Church brings in singing them. I have attended Mass at numerous parishes, for example, where we sang a sultry version of Psalm 130: "Out of the depths I call to you, Lord; / Lord hear my cry!" (Ps 130:1–2). The sorrow, the pleading, the desire for help that the Psalmist is expressing are misshaped by the music.

The reason that chant is appropriate for the psalms is that it enables us to attend to the words and respond with a "reasonable" offering of ourselves to Christ's speech. We are not inundated with a drum kit, the whimsy of a saxophonist, or the heavy-handed interpretation of a composer. Instead, it is the text that becomes clear to us. The words matter precisely because they are the speech of Christ, inviting us to unite ourselves more closely to the Word made flesh.

God woos us through the sweetness of his speech. We are not forced into anything through this relationship. In that sense, the psalms should give us time to savor God's speech, to make it our own, and eventually, to offer in love our very hearts.

LISTENING AND RESPONDING

Singing the psalms is also a way for us to embody the structure of the Mass as a whole. God calls. God speaks.

God acts. And then we respond with our voice as a gift to God. Having listened to the first reading, how can we not offer a sung response?

Our familiarity with listening to the psalms and responding in love need not be reserved simply to the Eucharistic liturgy. The psalms should become part of our homes. The Church's Liturgy of the Hours, which involves all the psalms of the Bible prayed over the course of a month, should be carried out by laypeople in the domestic sphere. The voice of the psalms will ring out not simply in the parish church but in our bedrooms, our kitchens, and our workplaces. Our children will memorize these psalms, able to take up Christ's voice wherever they are. We are given in the psalms a grammar for prayer, a way of speaking to God out of the fullness of our humanity.

A retrieval of a constant praying of the psalms is necessary for a robust sense of discipleship in the Church today. We do not encounter the person of Jesus simply within the affections that we want to cultivate. The Gospel is never simply about a false sense of happiness or joy, avoiding the rest of what it means to be human. The psalms move us outside of ourselves, forming us to take up Christ's voice of joy and sorrow as our own wherever we go. As Holly Taylor Coolman writes:

> The psalms will encourage believers to give voice to the passions—anger, guilt, despair— that are surely already at work in their lives. At the same time, the psalms will give words to speak those passions that move toward healing and wholeness. Over time, a body

of believers will be significantly shaped and formed.[12]

We learn to be fully human, and thus to become divine, through regular praying of the psalms. In this way, when we sing them at Mass, we are not simply engaging in a musical interlude. We are becoming the sacrifice of love that God intended us to be.

> I will extol you, my God and king;
>> I will bless your name forever.
> Every day I will bless you;
>> I will praise your name forever.
> Great is the LORD and worthy of high praise;
>> God's grandeur is beyond understanding.

(Ps 145:1–3)

QUESTIONS AND PRACTICES

1. Where in your life are you experiencing great joy? great sorrow? How might the psalms enable you to pray to God about this joy or sorrow?

2. How are the psalms sung at your parish? Are there ways that this singing could be improved? How so?

3. Make a commitment to read and meditate upon one psalm every day for 150 days straight. Keep a journal and write down what you discover in your prayer.

CHAPTER ELEVEN

Acclaiming the Gospel

"Worthy Is the Lamb That Was Slain"
(Rev 5:12)

Catholics do weird things with books. We paint them, creating illuminated images alongside the text. We kiss them, as if they are an encounter with our beloved spouse. We incense the Book of the Gospels and process with it alongside candles. Not once in my academic career have I have adored a copy of the complete works of William Shakespeare. Yet every Sunday, as the Book of the Gospels is processed from altar to ambo, I sing a hymn of praise to God.

What are we doing every Sunday? Why do we put smoke all over a book? Why do we adore it, kiss it, and even greet it as a dear friend of ours? It is, of course, because this book is no book. It is the presence of Jesus Christ in our midst.

THE PRESENCES OF JESUS CHRIST

Many Catholics know that Jesus Christ is really present in the Eucharist. Yet they seem less aware that Christ's presence at Mass unfolds in a variety of ways. At the Second

Vatican Council, the Church wrote about these various presences:

> Christ is always present in His Church, especially in her liturgical celebrations. He is present in the sacrifice of the Mass, not only in the person of His minister, "the same now offering, through the ministry of priests, who formerly offered himself on the cross," but especially under the Eucharistic species. By His power He is present in the sacraments, so that when a man baptizes it is really Christ Himself who baptizes. He is present in his word, since it is He Himself who speaks when the holy scriptures are read in the Church. He is present, lastly, when the Church prays and sings, for He promised: "Where two or three are gathered together in my name, there am I in the midst of them" (Mt 18:20).[13]

The procession with the Book of the Gospels is a ritual action in which we recognize the presence of Christ among us. We sing the *Alleluia*, and we take up with our lips the Gospel acclamation of the day. In the words of the Gospel read among us, Christ who has ascended into the heavens makes his presence known once again through speaking in the midst of the Church.

AN INTERRUPTIVE PRESENCE

What does this presence mean for us gathered to listen to the words of our Bridegroom, Jesus the Lord? We actually have to know something about what the Gospels are in the first place. They are strange texts, not immediately classifiable. To a certain extent they include biographical details about Jesus of Nazareth—where he came from, what he did, and what became of him. They reflect the faith of the Church about who Jesus really is, read through the lens of the Old Testament. They keep alive the memory of the crucified and risen Lord, passing it on from generation to generation.

In some ways, the heart of the Gospel, the Good News of Christ's victory over sin and death, is revealed in Mark 8. Jesus asks the disciples who they think he is. Peter answers that He is the Messiah. This is a loaded term in Israel's history. To be a Messiah is to be the anointed one, the King, the one who will restore authentic worship in the Temple and overthrow the Roman authorities. Everything that Jesus has done so far in the Gospel of Mark makes it seem like he is the Messiah. He has cured the sick, those who would be considered impure and outside the covenant. He teaches with authority. He has invited the Gentiles into the covenant, bringing all nations toward Israel. But then the Good News is turned upside down: "He began to teach them that the Son of Man must suffer greatly and be rejected by the elders, the chief priests, and the scribes, and be killed, and rise after three days" (Mk 8:31).

Peter can't take it. He objects. His understanding of what it means to be the Messiah doesn't include a crucified Lord. It doesn't include the Resurrection, the first fruits of our redemption. Peter is expecting a victory over the powers of Rome and is instead told that death itself will be slayed. Every one of the Gospels, each in its own way, reveals Jesus' victory over the powers of darkness.

They contemplate who he is, savoring the words that he uttered on mountaintops and in low valleys.

They conclude with the real hope that God's definitive victory has begun in the death and resurrection of Jesus Christ. And this victory means that everyone will soon be gathered to worship together at the mountain of the Lord: "A voice of one crying out in the desert: / 'Prepare the way of the Lord, / make straight his paths. / Every valley shall be filled / and every mountain and hill shall be made low. / The winding roads shall be made straight, / and the rough ways made smooth, / and all flesh shall see the salvation of God'" (Lk 3:4–6). This salvation has begun.

WORTHY ARE YOU, O LORD

If you're like me you may wonder why this Good News of salvation is not more immediately evident in the world. Wars still rage. Politicians still battle with one another, choosing the way of power over truth. We destroy the created world through pollution. We care little for the life of the unborn, the immigrant, the prisoner—all of those on the margins. People still get sick. They still die. If Jesus came to destroy sin and death, why are the vestiges of this darkness all around us?

The Book of Revelation provides images for us to contemplate relative to this problem. It is the slain Lamb, the image of Christ's very sacrifice itself, which is adored in the heavenly liturgy. As the tumult of the earth unfolds in the Book of Revelation (a text that is not a prediction of the end of the world), the power of heaven is revealed in the sacrificial Lamb: "Worthy is the Lamb that was slain / to receive power and riches, wisdom and strength, / honor and glory and blessing" (Rev 5:12). Craig R. Koester writes about this passage:

> The Lamb conquers by faithfully enduring death, and the result of this conquest is that people of every tribe, language, and nation are brought into new relationship with God. They are not degraded … but are elevated to membership in God's kingdom. Rather than being excluded from sacred service, they carry out sacred service to God.
>
> The dignity of being a priestly kingdom, which God gave to the tribes of Israel (Ex 19:16; Is 61:6), is extended to people of all tribes of the earth through the work of the Lamb. God's kingdom is not yet visible to the eye, but his people can be confident that they "will reign" (future tense) when God's purposes for the world are made complete in the new heavens and new earth (Rev 5:10; 22:5). Until that time, knowledge of belonging to God's kingdom offers a basis upon which to resist giving up in despair to the powers that oppose the reign of God.[14]

In gathering together to listen to the Gospel, we greet the presence of the slain Lamb who comes to break open the seals of the scroll. He comes to offer his interruptive presence, nourishing our imaginations once again, showing us what it means to belong to the kingdom of God. A lifetime of incensing and kissing and singing to a book, because we love the Bridegroom whose words echo in our Church, forms us to see God's kingdom coming into existence. Through hearing the Gospel, we are moved from despair at the power of the world and come to hear the voice of the Beloved Son, Jesus Christ, remind us that "Whoever wishes to come after me must deny himself, take up his cross, and follow me.... Whoever loses his life for my sake and that of the gospel will save it" (Mk 8:34–35).

ENSHRINING THE BOOK IN OUR HOMES

While it is important for us to read the Gospels outside of Church, to encounter in private prayer the risen Lord, it is also essential that we find a place in our homes to enshrine the Gospels as the living presence of the slain Lamb. In my own home, we keep a copy of the Saint John's Bible Book of the Gospels open to an illumination from the prologue of the Gospel of John. This is not simply for the sake of promoting attractive religious décor. Rather, we are reminded every time we enter our living room that the slain Lamb, the Word made flesh, still makes his voice known among us. The Gospels aren't folk tales of a wisdom figure of long ago. Jesus, the Lamb of God, reigns still. He reigns in our homes. He reigns in our hearts. He reigns in our parishes, and everywhere that the People of God proclaim the Good News that Jesus is Lord of heaven and earth.

Likewise, we keep icons of Jesus in prominent places on our walls. As we go to bed, we kiss these icons with our son. In doing this, we hope to form our son to see that Jesus is not an idea. He is a Person. He is the Bridegroom. The Jesus whom we adore at home is the very same Christ who speaks to us on Sunday mornings as the Gospel is read.

Come Lord Jesus,
fill the hearts of your faithful ones,
console us with your saving words,
and make us into a kingdom of priests to glorify God
from age to age.
Amen.

QUESTIONS AND PRACTICES

1. In acclaiming the Gospel at the beginning of Mass, we recognize the presence of Jesus in the Scriptures. What does this presence mean for your own praying of Scripture at home?

2. The presence of Jesus in the Gospels is interruptive. How have the words of Christ in the Gospel been a challenge for you?

3. The kingdom of God is at hand in the presence of Christ preaching and teaching among us. How has this presence of Christ brought you to a deeper understanding of what it means to be a disciple of the risen Lord?

4. Purchase a copy of the Bible that has art included within it (try, for example, the St. John's Bible, available at www.saintjohnsbible.org). Pray with this text every night as a family, leaving the page open for you to see when you come into your home.

CHAPTER TWELVE

The Homily

"Today This Scripture Passage Is Fulfilled in Your Hearing"
(Lk 4:21)

One need not be a negative ninny to recognize that preaching within the Church is not especially excellent. One Sunday, during a particularly atrocious act of preaching (which was also uniquely long), I took my infant son to the back of church because he was fussy. Also, because I was fussy. There I encountered father after father, mother after mother, who had also escaped from the church. Guilty for this fact, we remained silent, trying our best to avoid looking each other in the eye. We knew that our children could have remained at Mass, but we had to escape from the assault upon our ears that was unfolding at the front of the church.

It was not that we thought the preaching was unentertaining (and indeed, it was not entertaining). Rather, it never connected to the Gospel. It never connected to our lives. It never connected us to Christ. It was full of long stories about the priest's upbringing. His various roles he's served throughout the country and world. What he thought about a recent papal document. After forty-five minutes of meandering, the priest sat down. We returned to our pews, ready to resume the sacrifice of the Mass, each of us offering a silent hymn of thanksgiving that the homily had finally ended.

As laypeople, we cannot control the quality of preaching at Mass. But we can express to our pastors what we actually want to hear from preaching: the word of Christ wooing us toward a renewed commitment of love unto the end. Once we have a better understanding of what preaching should be—an encounter with the risen Lord inviting us to see how the kingdom of God is unfolding here and now—we can speak with our pastors and deacons about the role of the homily.

EXPECTATIONS FOR PREACHING

While it is certainly easier to blame bishops, priests, and deacons for preaching that fails to measure up, it's important that laypeople acknowledge our contribution to the problem. My undergraduates, for example, often see the best preachers as the most entertaining ones. The preacher who can't reference the latest Taylor Swift song or Pixar film is considered less effective. The homilist who doesn't tell the best jokes is considered second rate. Even if we don't admit it, there is something about us that wants to be entertained. And the standard of entertainment that we set up for the preaching act is almost too much for any cleric to bear. Be witty. Be spiritual. Be interesting. Be human. Also, speak words I've never heard before. New ones. Every week.

This is not ultimately what the Church had in mind when she emphasized the renewal of preaching at the Second Vatican Council. Indeed, the preacher needs a formation into a form of rhetoric that can communicate to us the gift of salvation. But it is often the case that we are demanding a degree of rhetorical excellence that too many of our young priests and deacons alike cannot fulfill (at least immediately). We also must have patience with one another. Perhaps the word that we find boring, unnecessary, unentertaining is actually engaging our fellow pilgrim in Christ's Body. We need patience, loving patience, with our homilists.

JESUS THE HOMILIST IN THE GOSPEL OF LUKE

That being said (was that enough patience?), it is also the case that our homilists need to find a new vision of preaching. They need further formation.

Perhaps we can look to the preaching of Jesus himself who, in the Gospel of Luke, functions as the homilist *par excellence.* The first homily Jesus gives in the Gospel of Luke is rather short. Standing in his hometown synagogue of Nazareth, he is invited to preach. He takes the scroll of Isaiah and reads a passage:

> "The Spirit of the Lord is upon me,
>> because he has anointed me
>>> to bring glad tidings to the poor.
> He has sent me to proclaim liberty to captives
>> and recovery of sight to the blind,
>>> to let the oppressed go free,
> and to proclaim a year acceptable to the Lord."
>
> Rolling up the scroll, he handed it back to the attendant and sat down, and the eyes of all in the synagogue looked intently at him. He

said to them, "Today this scripture passage is
fulfilled in your hearing." (Lk 4:18–20)

This is a boss move on the part of Jesus. He reads
to the assembly a passage describing how God's definitive reign has begun. The prophet Isaiah is announcing
that those outside the covenant are now going to be wel-
comed in. And Jesus, after a moment of silent contemplation, proclaims that this passage is fulfilled in his very
person. He is the great Jubilee of God in which prisoners
are freed, the sick are healed, and the world is re-created.
Jesus is the kingdom of God in a person.

In this, Jesus gives a vision of all future homilies.
The homily at Mass is not supposed to be about the
homilist, about a recent papal document (no matter
how important), or an upcoming capital campaign of
the parish. It is supposed to be about Jesus. It is supposed to be about how Jesus' enactment of the kingdom
of God is unfolding here and now among us. How the
Spirit of the risen Lord is fulfilling the promise to make
disciples of Christ in my parish, in my city, in my town,
in my state, in my country.

Of course, this means that the priest must be particular. Too often homilists speak general pious truths
without concretizing in the particulars of Christian life.
Don't just say it's hard to be a disciple. Deal with the
concrete difficulties of discipleship itself. Don't just say
that the culture is bad. Think with the assembly about
the ways that certain aspects of the culture make it difficult for us to recognize that Jesus is Lord. Don't just
exhort us to pray. Lead us toward prayer in the homily
itself, as we contemplate the wonders of what the Father

has done in Christ. Invite us to see how the history of salvation is being fulfilled (or not being fulfilled) right now among us.

Isn't this what happens in what is perhaps the Gospel of Luke's most famous homily? Two disciples, meandering on the road to Emmaus, encounter the risen Lord. They don't recognize him, and they share with Jesus their fear that the entire project that Jesus of Nazareth came to enact was just a giant waste of time. Don't we too feel like this sometimes? Sure, Jesus is supposed to be raised from the dead, but I still suffer from the wounds of sin and death. Sure, Christ is risen. But I'm unemployed and don't know what to do with my life. Jesus Christ comes to us and interprets for us the Scriptures:

> "Oh, how foolish you are! How slow of heart
> to believe all that the prophets spoke! Was it
> not necessary that the Messiah should suffer
> these things and enter into his glory?" Then
> beginning with Moses and all the prophets,
> he interpreted to them what referred to him
> in all the scriptures. (Lk 24:25–27)

The goal of the homilist is not simply to explain the Bible. It is not to report on the most recent findings in historical-critical scholarship. It is instead to show us the coherence of God's narrative of love. To show us once again that this narrative of love is present among us now, even if we're struggling to see it. And through this manifestation of what God has accomplished through Christ, we too are invited to recognize the glory of God made present in the poverty of what seems like bread and wine. Our hearts are to be warmed and, like the disciples, we are to run forth from our Eucharistic encounter and recount "what had taken place on the way and how he was made known to them in the breaking of the bread" (Lk 24:35).

THE SCRIPTURES AS DISCIPLESHIP FORMATION

In this sense, the homily is not simply for personal edification. It is meant to form the People of God as Eucharistic disciples heading forth to the margins of the world. The homily is not simply the responsibility of the priest to feed us with the Sacred Scriptures. Every one of us must develop a capacity to meditate on and proclaim the word of God to all the ends of the earth. As Pope Francis writes:

> Not only the homily has to be nourished by the word of God. All evangelization is based on that word, listened to, meditated upon, lived, celebrated and witnessed to. The sacred Scriptures are the very source of evangelization. Consequently, we need to be constantly trained in hearing the word. The Church does not evangelize unless she constantly lets herself be evangelized.[15]

We cannot let the homily be our only encounter with the Sacred Scriptures. Christ preaches to us every time we meditate on the Gospels. Christ preaches to us as we read sermons from the Fathers of the Church (easily found online). Christ preaches to us as we attend Bible studies, as we read commentaries, as we discuss Christ's presence in the word with fellow disciples in small groups.

It is often the case that you may still be bored by the homily. You may still find that the preaching of the priest is inadequate. The homilist may still be far too focused on himself rather than the presence of Jesus Christ dwelling among us. You don't have to leave the church. You don't have to find a new parish. Find a way to let the priest know that his preaching isn't working. Be very kind and be very honest.

At the same time, let your own imagination muse on the word of God in the midst of an atrocious homily. Get lost in stained glass windows and incense and frescoes on the wall. Go home and read Bernard of Clairvaux, Hildegard of Bingen, or John Henry Newman's preaching on the very same text. Don't feel powerless. For the word of God is active. It is alive. Christ still seeks to meet us through the Scriptures—even through the most impoverished of homilies. Look for him there. Often, in the midst of this boredom, you'll find a consoling word that renews your own commitment to the self-giving love of discipleship.

> Dear Jesus,
> send your Holy Spirit to me
> so that I may delight in every word in the Sacred
>   Scriptures.
> Teach me to long for your presence in my medita-
>   tion upon your Law.
> Give the Church holy preachers who offer to the
>   Church a word of transforming love.
> Make us into disciples who run forth from Mass
>   to proclaim to our friends, our neighbors, and

those who hate us the good news that God is love.

QUESTIONS AND PRACTICES

1. Imagine that you walk off the street and into your parish. What would you think about the homily? What would feed you? What would leave you hungry for more?

2. Read the Sunday readings for the week. Write down four or five points that you think might need to be included in a homily. How might these points lead you to an encounter with Christ?

3. How might your parish support prayerful study of the Scriptures for everyone in the parish? How would this study of the Bible lead to discipleship?

CHAPTER THIRTEEN

The Profession of Faith

"I Believe"

My students, almost universally, see the prayers they create using their own words as more authentic than the "rote" prayers they learned as children. Saying the Our Father is fine. But that prayer isn't my personal experience of who God is. If I really want to speak with Jesus, then I have to use my own speech. My own authentic words of praise given to the Lord.

This problem is even more acute when it comes to the Creed. Very few praise and worship songs rejoice in the consubstantiality of the Son with the Father. They don't get lost in wonder at the profession that the Spirit proceeds from the Father and the Son. These songs use a devotional register, which the Creed doesn't seem to possess. It's hard to imagine an assembly with hands raised high, clapping along, as they power their way through the Nicene Creed.

I would be lying if I said that I've found the Creed at Mass to be the pinnacle of my devotional life. While I often am led to tears by a Communion Motet, by the way that the sun refracts above the altar as incense ascends to the heavenly spheres, I am more often entirely unaware that I am saying the Creed at all. We begin. We end. I wonder what happened.

Yet my own lackluster proclamation of the Profession of Faith should not be the way that the Church decides what is important in the Mass. In fact, if we attend to the Creed in the Mass, its role in bringing together all believers into one faith and one baptism, we will start to understand that to profess the Creed at Mass is a supreme act of love to the God who first loved us.

ONE FAITH, ONE LORD, ONE BAPTISM

In the earliest stages of the history of the Mass, the Creed was not professed. The original place of the Creed, whatever version was used, was in the context of baptism. The Creed would be given to the elect (those entering their final preparation for the sacraments of initiation) in secret, and a week later, the elect would return the Creed. From very early in the history of the Church, the Creed is tied to our identity as Christians. The Christian is the one who believes these things about God, and thus has conformed one's life to the truths proclaimed in the Creed.

And what are these truths? At Mass, there are two options to use for the Profession of Faith. The first is the Nicene Creed, finding its final form in 381. The second is the Apostles' Creed, an older Creed that should be used especially during the seasons of Lent and Easter because it is the baptismal creed *par excellence*.

In both Creeds, we profess faith in the triune God: Father, Son, and Holy Spirit. To get what's going on in the Creed, you have to read it kind of like a story. There is one God, the Father, who has created heaven and earth.

This Father is the source of all life, all love. He is gift. He is love. We encounter this radical love in the Old Testament, learning to see God as the Bridegroom of the bridal nation of Israel: "You shall be my people, and I will be your God" (Ez 36:28).

The full sense of what it means to say "Father" was revealed by the Father's Son, Jesus Christ. Jesus is not just sort of God or kind of God. He is "God from God, Light from Light, true God from true God, begotten, not made, consubstantial with the Father...." This means that when we meet the face of the Son in Jesus Christ, we are really encountering God. It is God who empties himself, being born in the poverty of Bethlehem. It is God who fasts in the desert. It is God who heals the sick. It is God who dies on the cross and is raised three days later. It is God, who is truly human, who ascends into heaven and will come to offer divine judgment of the living and the dead.

And this "sonship" of Jesus actually matters for us Christians. We are baptized in the name of the Father, the Son, and the Holy Spirit. We become sons and daughters of the Father; brothers and sisters of Jesus, the Son. As Joseph Ratzinger (later, Pope Benedict XVI) writes:

> Becoming a Christian means sharing in Jesus' prayer, entering into the model provided by his life, that is, the model of his prayer. Becoming a Christian means saying "Father" with Jesus and, thus, becoming a child, God's son—God—in the unity of the Spirit, who allows us to be ourselves and precisely in this way draws us into the unity of God. Being a

Christian means looking at the world from this central point, which gives us freedom, hope, decisiveness, and consolation.[16]

To get Jesus "right" is to actually get our salvation right. We are saved by entering into the sonship of Jesus. We are saved by receiving everything that we have from the Father and offering back to the Father the entirety of our wills as an act of love. All of this is possible because of the Holy Spirit, the love of the Father and the Son, who has "spoken through the prophets" and now speaks in the interior of our own hearts.

This is the God who is alive and active in the Church. This is the God who forgives our sins, renewing in us our baptism as priests, prophets, and kings in the world. This is the God who will raise us from the dead, completing the transformation of creation that began in the resurrection of the Son. This is the God whom we will enjoy when we are taken up into heaven. This is our one Lord. This is our one faith. This is the common baptism that we share.

THE EUCHARIST AND SONSHIP

Josef Jungmann notes that it is very appropriate that the Creed entered into the Mass, even if it was not original to it. He writes:

In the reawakening of all those concepts of our faith which center on Christ's life-work, in that reawakening with which every celebration of the Eucharist must begin, that reawakening which is the prime purpose of the whole reading service … in that reawakening the Credo has become a main element.[17]

Right before we begin the Liturgy of the Eucharist, we are invited to remember why we can pray this liturgy at all. We can pray the Eucharistic Prayer as the Church because Christ has invited us to share in his sonship. Catechumens (those who are unbaptized yet preparing to enter the Church) are dismissed from the Mass after the homily and before the Creed, because they do not yet share in the fullness of this sonship.

In a real way, the Creed reminds every Christian at Mass of the office that we occupy as those baptized into the name of the Father, the Son, and the Holy Spirit. We are sons and daughters of the living God. We can pray with confidence before the Father. The fullness of our initiation is the celebration of the Eucharist where we offer that sacrifice of praise that renews the world.

THE CREED AS OUR BRIDAL SPEECH

In this sense, the Creed does consist of our words. They are the words that the Church has handed on to us. These words, this symbol of our faith, is the gift that the Church has given to us in Baptism, in Confirmation, and in the Eucharist. We are sons and daughters of the Son. Every time we profess the Creed at Mass, it is almost like we are renewing our marriage vows with the Bridegroom. I will be yours. You are mine.

> Breathe on me, Holy Spirit,
> Refreshing me as a child of the Father.
> Teach me to pray like Jesus, the Word made flesh.

Give me his mind, his heart, and his will
so that I may offer my mind, my heart, and my
 will
as a sacrifice of praise to the Father.
Amen.

QUESTIONS AND PRACTICES

1. What parts of the Creed have you had the most difficulty understanding? How has focusing on the Creed as a story helped you in understanding what you profess every week at Mass?

2. Thinking about the Creed as a vow changes the way we might recite it at Mass. How have you lived up to the vows you profess in the Creed? How have you become like Jesus Christ, the Son?

3. For the next week, slowly profess the Creed during your prayer time or before going to bed. How has this changed the way that you pray the Creed at Mass?

CHAPTER FOURTEEN

The Universal Prayer

"Let Us Pray to the Lord"

Passive-aggressive public prayer is one of my favorites. When I was an undergraduate seminarian, the priest celebrating daily Mass would often open up the floor for any prayers of the faithful that we might offer. While most seminarians didn't take the bait to increase the length of Mass (since seminary homilies were often already very long), every few weeks there would be a prayer war. One seminarian would pray for the end of all war and forgiveness for all soldiers who took a life. Another seminarian would pray for the protection of the military and the success of their mission.

I would often imagine these prayer wars moving from passive-aggressive to aggressive-aggressive. "For all those who are annoying and lack a sense of good order, especially Tom...." "For all those who are incapable of having a complete thought and probably should be asked to leave the seminary, especially Carlos...."

Of course, this is not the only way the Universal Prayer, also called the Prayer of the Faithful, can go wrong. Participating in a variety of on-campus groups that assembled the prayers together, I was in a position to assess what prayers we should offer. "For all members

of the Church who are thinking through a religious vocation, whether as married or lay, in some part of the country, where there is a need for those vocations, and other
vocations too, which are also important. Let us pray to
the Lord...." I would often muse to myself, "I *think* I pray
to the Lord."

It should not be shocking that the Universal Prayer
is one of those soft spots in the Mass where human cre-
ativity often detracts from really praying. In order to get
the Universal Prayer "right," we have to figure out why it's
there at all. Likewise, we need to ask ourselves what we
should be praying for.

THE UNIVERSAL PRAYER

Before the Second Vatican Council, there was no Universal Prayer in the Mass of the Roman Rite. After the
Creed came the Offertory Prayers. But at the Council, the
Fathers explicitly asked that the Universal Prayer be returned to the Mass:

> Especially on Sundays and feasts of obliga-
> tion there is to be restored, after the Gospel
> and the homily, "the common prayer" or
> "the prayer of the faithful." By this prayer, in
> which the people are to take part, interces-
> sion will be made for holy Church, for the
> civil authorities, for those oppressed by vari-
> ous needs, for all mankind, and for the salva-
> tion of the entire world.[18]

In light of what we said about the Creed in the
previous chapter, the restoration of the Universal Prayer
makes sense. The Christian has a vocation to enter into

Christ's prayer for the entire world. At the Eucharistic liturgy, the world is not left behind. We do not escape history but rather bring it to the altar of salvation. We pray for the Church and for her leaders. We pray for the nation that it may care for the common good. We pray for those who are suffering in the world through natural disasters, because of illness, because of loneliness and other sorrows. We pray for women and men of good will. We pray that everyone might enter into the life of the Church.

The *General Instruction of the Roman Missal* (the Church's official theological, pastoral, and liturgical instruction on how to pray the Mass) gives a structure that the prayer should follow: the needs of the Church, for public authorities and the salvation of the world, those burdened by difficulties, and the local community praying this day.[19] The prayers should be short, brief, and expressive of the community's own prayer. The deacon or a cantor, a lector, or one of the faithful are to read the prayers from the ambo. And the congregation may respond to these prayers either through silence or an appropriate invocation (which is not prescribed).

The Universal Prayer of the Church, for this reason, should not be "opened up" to the general community. Instead, it is assumed that on Sundays and feast days the prayer has been written and formed with the community's needs in mind. It is not to be written by the priest at the last minute. It is not to be written by a committee in which each member inserts his or her own particular interest. It is to be written in a structured way so that we can recall the needs of the world before we pray at the altar.

HISTORY MATTERS

The Prayers of the Faithful represent a vision of the Christian in the world that should not be forgotten by the Mass-goer. We don't leave behind our material and historical realities when we go to Mass. We don't go to Mass to escape from the sorrows of the world, as if Church is a safe haven from politics, from illness, and from suffering. Nor for that matter should the Church simply become a part of the world. Instead, through the intercessions that we offer, we really bring the material world before God the Father, asking it to be transformed in the Mass that we celebrate. In these intercessions we want the Church, the world, the entirety of our lives to become what it should be in the kingdom of God.

The Orthodox theologian Alexander Schmemann has something to say to us Roman Catholics on this point. He writes:

> If "assembling as the Church" presupposes separation from the world ... this exodus from the world is accomplished *in the name of the world*, for the sake of its salvation. For we are flesh of the flesh and blood of the blood of this world. We are a part of it, and only by us and through us does it ascend to its Creator, Savior and Lord, to its goal and fulfillment. We separate ourselves from the world in order to bring it, in order to lift it up to the kingdom, to make it once again the way to God and participation in his eternal kingdom.[20]

We pray for the world as the Church not because we hate the world. Not in a way that says that the world is here, and we're there, and the two should never meet. Rather, we enter into the Mass, we separate from the world for an hour or so, so that we can offer prayers for the world. So that the world might be restored to what God intended it to be: a place of divine praise.

In this way, the Universal Prayer reveals to us our vocation as lay Catholics in the world. We are to bring everything to the altar of God. Our priesthood, which is baptismal and not ministerial, is nonetheless a real intercession before God for the sake of the world. We are not just offering quaint little prayers. We are not creating intercessions that enable us to express our political position at Mass. Instead, we are really inviting God to transform everything in love.

> We pray for the Holy Father that he might serve as a sign of unity to all Christians. Lord hear us: *Lord, graciously hear us.*
>
> We pray for all those Christians undergoing persecution throughout the world. That civil authorities will protect them from violence. Lord hear us: *Lord, graciously hear us.*
>
> We pray for all those preparing to be married in the Church. May their formation prepare them to become a living sign of the love between Christ and the Church. Lord hear us: *Lord, graciously hear us.*
>
> We pray for the poor that your Church may go forth to meet your Christ among

those on the margins of our society. Lord hear us: *Lord, graciously hear us.*

We pray for our local community. May it become a civilization of love where women and men come to know the gracious goodness of God. Lord hear us: *Lord, graciously hear us.*

QUESTIONS AND PRACTICES

1. The Universal Prayer signifies that we are to bring the entire world to the altar of God. What does this mean for the vocation of a Catholic in the world?

2. Write your own Prayer of the Faithful for your family or your roommates. What have you chosen to pray for? Why?

3. How might your parish improve how it prays the Universal Prayer?

CHAPTER FIFTEEN

The Preparation of the Gifts

"My Father Was a Wandering Aramean"
(Dt 26:5)

It was time to propose to my girlfriend. I should have felt joy, but instead I was anxious. I wasn't afraid of the commitment. I wasn't trembling before the possibility that she would say no (we had talked about getting married many times). No, I was afraid of buying a ring. How was I to make a decision when my previous knowledge of jewelry was mostly reserved to the candy necklaces that I played with as a child?

My first trip to the jewelry store did not go especially well. The saleswoman taught me the four Cs: cut, clarity, carat, and color. Then she began to talk to me about God, having learned that I was studying theology at Notre Dame. "Did you know," she said without any irony, "that diamonds are the culmination of God's creation. The bigger the diamond you purchase, the more you'll show your love of God and your spouse." I left.

The second store was worse. The woman showed me some rings. I announced what was my rather insignificant graduate student budget for said ring. Then the saleswoman suggested the way that I should propose, seemingly unaware that I was capable of figuring out what she was doing. "On Sweetest Day," she said, "take your girlfriend to dinner. Slide a box across the table, giving her a pearl necklace. Just as she is overcome with emotion, slide the ring across the table and tell her that you love her and want to spend the rest of your life with her." Interesting, I thought to myself. Your proposal idea would involve me purchasing an additional item from you. I left.

Of course, eventually I did find a place to purchase a ring where diamonds were not praised as the pinnacle of God's creation and where the salesperson didn't try to swindle me into purchasing additional jewelry to celebrate a fake holiday. The absurdity of both attempted sales revealed to me something about the inadequacy of our understanding of gift. Both saleswomen, in their own way, seemed to see the engagement ring not as a gift of love but as an economic exchange. The bigger ring, the more expensive ring—that will buy love. The engagement ring, meant to serve as a sign of commitment, of self-gift, became part of an economy of exchange. I give so that I might receive.

THE MASS AND THE GIFT

A very different sense of gift operates in the Mass. As the Roman Missal says in its instructions for the offertory, "It is desirable that the faithful express their participation by making an offering, bringing forward bread and wine for the celebration of the Eucharist and perhaps other gifts to relieve the needs of the Church and of the poor." At Mass, we do bring forth gifts. We bring forth bread and wine, money and food to feed the poor. We bring forth our very bodies as an offering of love. But we are not giving these gifts as an economic exchange. We are not saying to God (except perhaps in the privacy of our hearts), "Hey, I'm at Mass. Do something for me!"

The proper sense of offering a gift at Mass is revealed in the Old Testament. In Deuteronomy, God, through Moses, gives instructions for offering a thanksgiving sacrifice in light of a successful harvest. The first fruits of the harvest are to be given to the priest. The one offering this gift, a costly one because you never know if there will be other fruits, is to say:

> "My father was a wandering Aramean who went down to Egypt with a small household and lived there as an alien. But there he became a nation great, strong and numerous. When the Egyptians maltreated and oppressed us, imposing hard labor upon us, we cried to the LORD, the God of our fathers, and he heard our cry and saw our affliction, our toil and our oppression. He brought us out of Egypt with his strong hand and outstretched arm, with terrifying power, with signs and wonders; and bringing us into this country, he gave us this land flowing with milk and honey. Therefore, I have now brought the first fruits of the products of the soil which you, O LORD, have given me." (Dt 26:5–10)

The speaker of this prayer is not buttering God up. Rather, there is a real sense in which the one offering the first fruits is acknowledging that nothing he gives is actually his to begin with. He should not exist at all. His existence as a member of Israel, a holy nation, is gift. His liberation from the slavery of Egypt is pure gift. The land of milk and honey, the land that has produced these first fruits, is gift. Nothing is his to begin with.

DISPOSING OURSELVES TO DISPOSSESSION

The Offertory at Mass, therefore, is really not simply about us bringing things forward to God. It's an image of the kind of dispossession that we need to practice. Over the course of any day, through the effect of sin, we may forget that everything we are, everything we have, is gift. We may pass by the homeless man or woman on the street, ignoring their suffering. We may stop praying each morning to God, instead jumping right into our busy workload. We may ignore our children, our spouse, focusing entirely on our own career. We may develop a relationship with God where we only pray when we really want something.

What God wants at every Mass is not an economic exchange. God wants us—the entirety of our hearts, our minds, and our wills offered on the altar. The Offertory prepares us to give ourselves over as an act of love in response to the love that God has already offered to us. To the gifts that God has already bestowed. The Anglican theologian Evelyn Underhill writes about offering ourselves at Mass:

> The beginning of that Eucharistic life, which is the true life of the Church and each of her members, is such a free and unconditional self-offering of the created life to that trans-

forming energy which is even now at work on us. We are to offer in simplicity what we are and what we have to the eternal purposes of God; without any self-occupied attempt to determine its precise quality and value.[21]

In this sense, the Mass is a deeply countercultural activity. We tend to measure the importance of every human being according to their contribution to the economy, their political power, the extent of their education, their physical beauty. None of this matters at Mass. What matters is that we come forth to the altar of God, giving whatever we have, whoever we are. Bread and wine are offered. Money is brought forward. But along with this bread and wine, you and I, in all of our imperfections are also placed upon that altar.

THE PRACTICE OF LEARNING TO GIVE

This offering of ourselves is no easy task. We won't learn to perform it to perfection just by going to Mass. Rather, we have to live a life of gift every single day. There can be very concrete ways that we do this.

Like many Millennials, I am addicted to my smartphone. I check it frequently to see if I have an email; if someone has written on my Facebook wall; if one of my very many witty Tweets has been retweeted the appropriate number of times (follow me @timothypomalley). Again and again, I stare at that screen.

But this practice of staring at the screen turns me inward. I am only thinking about myself, my universe, when I look at the smartphone. I do not hear the voice of my wife, asking me a question. I do not hear my child, asking me to play with him. I'm too busy. I'm too distracted by myself.

The practice of offering ourselves at Mass can begin at a very human level. Start offering your very real attention on a daily basis to those around you. Put down your iPhone when you're talking to someone. Lock cell phones in a drawer at dinner. Spend Sundays as a Sabbath day, avoiding the phone altogether. In each case, we will find ourselves more capable of seeing every moment of our lives as a gift to be received. We will start paying attention to what we're grateful for, rather than escaping into our digital universe. We may find ourselves offering prayers throughout the day, instead of turning with boredom to our phones.

In addition, it is not unimportant that we give our money at Mass. Americans keep their incomes private. After all, it's my money. But to give away some of our money, enough money that it actually hurts a bit, is a reminder that everything that we have is a gift. That it's actually not our money to begin with—but money intended to serve the needs of the poor.

But even the money is still a sign of something else. It is not a sign that we're supergenerous, worthy of being praised for our remarkable stewardship. It is a sign that we're willing to give everything. I'm willing to give over my very self, everything that I have, to the living God.

> Take, Lord, and receive all my liberty,
> my memory, my understanding,
> and my entire will,
> All I have and call my own.
> You have given all to me.
> To you, Lord, I return it.

Everything is yours; do with it what you will.
Give me only your love and your grace,
that is enough for me.
(Ignatius of Loyola, *Suscipe*)

QUESTIONS AND PRACTICES

1. What obstacles in the modern world prevent Catholics from seeing everything as a gift? What might you do to remove these obstacles?

2. The Catholic life is learning to say thank you. How does your regular practice of attending Mass help you to see your life as a gift? Where do you struggle with this?

3. In a prayer journal, write down three things every day that you are thankful for. Do this for a month. Name these things in your heart during the offertory at Sunday Mass. How has this practice changed your prayer?

4. Review your budget, considering what you give each week at Mass during the offertory. Could you give more? How much more?

CHAPTER SIXTEEN

The Prayer Over the Offerings

"Blessed Are You, Lord"

I often find myself annoyed at being a creature. When I get sick, instead of treating it as part of being human, I see it as something that I should be able to conquer through sheer force of will. When I'm tired, I counteract the effects of the exhaustion by pumping myself with caffeine. When I look into the mirror, discovering the creeping presence of crow's feet and gray hair, I want to stop the aging process, wishing that I could exist forever as a twenty-five-year-old.

But in the end, we are creatures among creatures. And the Mass necessitates that we remember this. We are part of the created world. It is creation itself that is offered to God. Therefore, at every Mass we are taught that we are indeed blessed creatures of a God who has great plans for the entire created order.

FORGETTING OUR CREATURELINESS

It's not actually easy for us to think about ourselves as dependent creatures living within a world in which we share relationships with the rest of creation. In the Industrial Revolution, we discovered that we could master creation. Think about air travel, for example. The human being is thus far incapable of traveling on one's own at five hundred miles per hour. Yet with air travel, we have conquered time and space itself. We can leave New York and arrive in London a mere six hours later. A journey that would have taken our forebears a month, full of trials, now takes no more than an evening.

Likewise, one might consider electric light. Two hundred years ago, our days were organized around the rising and the setting sun. You could not work the farm after dark because you could not see. We were deeply connected to the rhythms of the day. In today's world, as soon as darkness descends, I turn on a light and it's bright as day in my home.

My point is not to decry technological innovation as if it is something terrible. These advances have extended our lives and made us capable of connecting with one another across great distances. But the underbelly of this advancement has been a forgetfulness among human beings that we are actually dependent on creation. We are created beings among created beings. We are not gods of the universe.

BLESSING CREATION

After the gifts are brought forward, the Church reminds us that we are indeed part of a broader created order. The priest prays: "Blessed are you, Lord God of all creation, / for through your goodness we have received / the bread we offer you: / fruit of the earth and work of human hands, / it will become for us the bread of life." In some ways, this is a strange prayer. After all, in a few moments the bread and the wine will be consecrated.

It will become Christ's Body, Christ's Blood. Why draw our attention to the matter before us as bread? Why thank God a couple of seconds later for the "fruit of the vine and work of human hands" that will "become our spiritual drink." Isn't the wine simply important as the blood of Christ?

This style of prayer, performed over the Eucharistic elements of bread and wine, is an old one. It is called a *Berakah* (Blessing) prayer. Israel used to thank God for everything in this fashion. During morning prayers, Israel would pray: "You are blessed, Lord our God, King of the universe, 'you who form the light, and create the darkness' (Is 45:7); who shed the light of your mercy upon the earth and those who dwell on it; who, out of goodness constantly renew every day the works of your creation."[22]

The purpose of this kind of prayer was to transform every moment of one's day into a thanksgiving offering. These prayers were often attuned to everything in creation. There were prayers of gratitude for the rising sun, for the food that we received, for the sleep that we would enjoy.

The Second Vatican Council included a *Berakah* prayer during the offering as a way of drawing our own attention to the gift of the created order. The bread that we offer is already blessed, even before it is consecrated. It is blessed because it comes forth from produce that is a gift of God. It comes forth from the work of human hands that take the gift of wheat and transform it into bread. Bread's origins within material creation are already a sign of what it will become in the Eucharist—a transformed gift.

Likewise, wine comes forth from the gift of grapes that we have received. It is a product of human effort. And the delight that we take in enjoying wine, savoring it, is a foretaste of the Eucharistic banquet itself.

In this sense, the blessing prayers offered over the gifts of bread and wine return us to something that we should never forget. The Mass is not leaving the rest of the world behind. It is not escaping creation. Rather, at Mass we offer the gift of creation back to God. Creation returns to its original vocation as sacred matter to be offered to God. The Mass gradually teaches us to read creation, all of it, as a sign of God's providential love.

THE VOCATION OF BREAD, OUR VOCATION

Indeed, bread and wine are important precisely as items of food that we bring before God. They are signs of life itself, the life that we are to offer on the altar. As Alexander Schmemann writes:

> We already know that food is life, that it is the very principle of life and that the whole world has been created as food for man. We also know that to offer this food, this world, this life to God is the initial "Eucharistic" function of man, his very fulfillment as man. We know that we were created as celebrants of the sacrament of life, of its transformation into life in God, communion with God. We know that real life is "eucharist," a movement of love and adoration towards God, the movement in which alone the meaning and value of all that exists can be revealed and fulfilled.[23]

Bread finds its perfect vocation on the altar. So, too, do we as human beings. Our vocation is to be priests in the world. This doesn't mean that every one of us is ordained to preside at Mass. We are priests because we are meant to bring all of creation back to God as a sacrifice of love.

For this reason, it is precisely our interrelationship with creation that matters. We can't think of ourselves as individuals apart from the created order. We belong together. We are the priests who bring forth married love and children before God as an act of praise. We are the priests who create art and music, and offer it back to God. We are the priests who garden and care for our home, creating a civilization of love.

At Mass, we learn what our vocation is: to be priests within the created order. The blessing prayers at the beginning of the offertory remind us of this vocation, of the responsibility that we have to be creatures. And we offer all of creation, which is gift itself, back to God as a sacrifice of love. The priest reminds us of this as we enter into the Eucharistic Prayer. He prays, "Pray, brothers and sisters, that my sacrifice and yours may be acceptable to God, the almighty Father." The entire assembly, with the priest acting in the person of Christ, is to offer the sacrifice of the Mass. The vocation of every baptized person is a genuine participation in Christ's priesthood of self-giving love. We must learn to see all creation as a gift if we are to offer this sacrifice.

The Prayer over the Offerings underlines this priestly vocation of human beings as part of the created order. Sure, what we bring forth is bread and wine. Yet, as bread and wine it can become an efficacious sign that enables us to love Christ anew. To live out the Christian life more fully. As we pray on the Thirty-second Sunday in Ordinary Time:

> Look with favor, we pray, O Lord,
> upon the sacrificial gifts offered here,
> that, celebrating in mystery the Passion of your
> Son,
> we may honor it with loving devotion.

These created gifts, through God's favor, are to become the way that we adore more fully Christ's Paschal sacrifice. Bread and wine, as part of the very same created world that we belong to, can become for us an instrument that forms us to love God more fully.

THE GIFT OF SABBATH

One particular practice that might remind us that we are part of the created order is attending to practices of Sabbath rest. At the conclusion of *Laudato Si'*, Pope Francis does not simply suggest setting up practical ways to conserve creation. He speaks about the importance of the Sunday Sabbath in learning to see creation in a different light:

> On Sunday, our participation in the Eucharist has special importance. Sunday, like the Jewish Sabbath, is meant to be a day which heals our relationships with God, with ourselves, with others and with the world. Sunday is the day of the Resurrection, the "first day" of the new creation, whose first fruits are the Lord's risen humanity, the pledge of

the final transfiguration of all created reality. It also proclaims "man's eternal rest in God" (CCC 2175). In this way, Christian spirituality incorporates the value of relaxation and festivity. We tend to demean contemplative rest as something unproductive and unnecessary, but this is to do away with the very thing which is most important about work: its meaning. We are called to include in our work a dimension of receptivity and gratuity, which is quite different from mere inactivity. Rather, it is another way of working, which forms part of our very essence. It protects human action from becoming empty activism; it also prevents that unfettered greed and sense of isolation which make us seek personal gain to the detriment of all else. The law of weekly rest forbade work on the seventh day, "so that your ox and your donkey may have rest, and the son of your maidservant, and the stranger, may be refreshed" (Ex 23:12). Rest opens our eyes to the larger picture and gives us renewed sensitivity to the rights of others. And so the day of rest, centered on the Eucharist, sheds its light on the whole week, and motivates us to greater concern for nature and the poor.[24]

The hour spent at Sunday Mass is not enough time to practice the gift that God has revealed in Christ. Our Sundays are to be times of festivity, of sharing our lives with creation and one another. We should spend time together in the outdoors, rejoicing in the goodness of creation. We should make time for conversation, for eating with one another at the Sunday table. We should spend our time with the poor, not simply carrying out works of charity, but offering genuine hospitality to those who are Christ's presence among us.

Sunday is not just another day. It is that day that we offer back to God as a gift, a sign that we are creatures returning our time, our bodies, even our entire lives to God. If we practice Sunday rest well, then we will come to Mass well aware of the gift of bread and wine. The gift of being human beings, who offer to God a sacrifice of praise.

> Lord,
> help me to see all of creation as gift.
> May I offer you praise as my day unfolds.
> As I eat and work, as I spend my time with my
>   family, as I sleep in the evening.
> Give me the grace of the Spirit to see even sorrow
>   itself as a gift that draws me
> closer to the suffering of our Lord.
> Let me remember that I am a creature and not the
>   Creator.
> Let me remember the shortness of my life, and let
>   me spend this life at service of
> you, the God who is love.
> Amen.

QUESTIONS AND PRACTICES

1. What do you see as a gift in your life? What do you struggle to recognize as a gift? How might the Mass help you in this regard?

2. Choose five times during the day when you will give praise to God for the gift of your life. Write a short prayer for each of these times and pray these prayers every day.

3. How do you practice the Sabbath rest on Sunday? What makes it difficult? How might you better celebrate the gift of Sunday in your life?

4. Commit yourself to avoid all emailing and Internet use on the Sabbath. Use this time to spend with family or friends.

CHAPTER SEVENTEEN

The Roman Canon

The Roman Canon, or the First Eucharistic Prayer, is not often prayed in our parishes. For example, one parish that I belonged to timed the Mass to see if they could get everyone out in under an hour. That would include up to ten minutes of preaching, music, and the Eucharistic Prayer. For that reason, the parish never chose Eucharistic Prayer I, the Roman Canon, as an option. It was too long.

Canon means the "rule" by which one determines whether something measures up. In the case of Roman Catholicism, the Roman Canon is the Eucharistic Prayer that serves as the "rule" by which to make sense of the Church's Eucharistic praying as a whole. The goal of the Eucharistic Prayer is not simply to decorate the Institution narrative, those words of Christ at the Last Supper that the Church today understands as the consecration. Rather, the Eucharistic Prayer "performs" what the Eucharist is supposed to do: uniting together all the baptized into the unity of Christ's Body so that we may pray before the Father through the Son in the unity of the Holy Spirit for the salvation of the world.

A THEOLOGY OF THE EUCHARIST

Before attending to the Roman Canon itself, which is a rather structured prayer, it is important to understand what the Church says about the Eucharist as a sacrament. Here, the theologian St. Thomas Aquinas is helpful.

St. Thomas, in his *Summa Theologica*, addresses the various names given to the Eucharist.[25] Some call the Mass a sacrifice. Others call it Communion or the Greek word *Synaxis*, meaning assembly. Still others, Viaticum. For St. Thomas, these various names represent the "temporalities" of the Mass: past, present, and future. The Mass is a sacrifice insofar as it is a real commemoration of Christ's Passion. The Mass recalls a past and makes it present.

At the same time, it is Communion not simply with Jesus Christ but with the entire Church. The Mass calls the Church into being, into the unity of love that is our source and summit. The gathering of the Church is an authentic communion which culminates in our eating and drinking of Christ's Body and Blood.

It is also called Viaticum because it is bread for the journey that points toward our future: total enjoyment of God. The Mass is not simply about Jesus' presence here and now. It is a recollection of what Christ accomplished in his death and resurrection, which points toward our future with the Father, the Son, and the Holy Spirit.

Although the Roman Canon may seem like a strange prayer to the listener, it actually "performs" this Eucharistic theology in our midst. We are invited into the past of Christ's sacrifice made present among us. We enter into the present reality of communion, which is the life of the Church. And we receive a foretaste of union with the saints, who join us in our song of praise.

In the next chapter, I will draw our attention to each part of Eucharistic Prayers II, III, and IV. In this chapter, however, I simply want to point the reader to three features of the Roman Canon that help us make sense of every Eucharistic Prayer.

1. An emphasis on sacrifice throughout the Prayer.
2. The importance of repetition in the Canon.
3. The Canon's recalling of the living and the dead, the saints and the Church here on earth.

SACRIFICE IN THE ROMAN CANON

For Catholics, the Mass is a recalling of and making present of Christ's sacrifice on the cross. You do not need to be even that attentive to the Prayer to notice the prevalence of sacrifice throughout the Canon. The first words that the priest prays in Eucharistic Prayer I or the Roman Canon:

> To you, therefore, most merciful Father,
> we make humble prayer and petition
> through Jesus Christ, your Son, our Lord:
> that you accept
> and bless + these gifts, these offerings,
> these holy and unblemished sacrifices.

The bread and the wine on the altar are already pointing to the Passion of Christ. This is underlined by the way the priest makes the Sign of the Cross over the gifts of bread and wine as he recalls their identity as gifts, offerings, sacrifices presented to the Father. This understanding of the Mass has even been represented in Catholic art. Historically, the *Te igitur*, or very first two words in the Roman Canon, would have been represented by an image of the crucifix. The "T" of *Te* becomes Christ sacrificed on the cross. From the very beginning, the Eucharistic Prayer is a sacrificial prayer.

Yet what does it mean to think about the Eucharistic Prayer as a "sacrificial" prayer. We get the wrong idea if we think about the Church continually killing Jesus on the cross at every Mass. Christ's sacrifice is once and for all. We cannot repeat what Jesus did on Calvary. We cannot raise the Son of God from the dead. This marvelous event has happened, and it is precisely that it has happened that we can celebrate the Mass at all.

It is important to remember that the Mass is a "sacramental" memorial of Christ's death and resurrection. A sacrament, in the Church, is an efficacious sign instituted by Christ and entrusted to the Church whereby divine life is dispensed.[26] The sacrifice of Christ is made present to us once again through the signs of bread and wine that become Christ's Body and Blood. This presence is possible because the sacrifice in question has never ended. Christ's self-giving love on the cross is his deepest identity as the Son of the Father. He gives out of love to God. He gives out of love to us. And now the crucified and risen Lord reigns in heaven. His sacrifice of love continues even now, as the sacrifice of the cross passes over into the drama of the altar.

Sacrifice, for the Church, is not fundamentally about pain. It's not fundamentally about suffering. Rather, sacrifice is love. At every Mass, we participate in the sacrifice of God's love. We become actors in this drama. As Benedict XVI writes:

> The Eucharist draws us into Jesus' act of self-oblation. More than just statically receiving

the incarnate Logos, we enter into the very dynamic of his self-giving. The imagery of marriage between God and Israel is now realized in a way previously inconceivable: it had meant standing in God's presence, but now it becomes union with God through sharing in Jesus' self-gift, sharing in his body and blood. The sacramental "mysticism," grounded in God's condescension towards us, operates at a radically different level and lifts us to far greater heights than anything that any human mystical elevation could ever accomplish.[27]

The sacrifice of the Mass is not about watching some event unfold before us. It is about participating in God's own logic of love, becoming this love for the world. Logic is coherence. At Mass, by celebrating this sacrifice, we are saying that the coherence of the world, what makes sense of creation, is God's love revealed on the cross now present among us. We find our greatest sense of happiness in coming to the Eucharist and preparing to participate in this sacrifice. As Kimberly Belcher, commenting on this passage from Benedict XVI, writes: "To participate in this self-offering is the best human beings can do, and all that they can do, and the fulfillment of human nature!"[28]

This sacrifice of self-offering, participating in Jesus' sacrifice, is transformative of what it means to be human. For years, my wife and I went to Mass suffering with the pain of infertility. We could barely look around us because every time we did, we encountered families who seemed so happy, our friends, who seemed to be able to procreate at the drop of a hat. And there we were, desiring to have a child, but unable to conceive.

At Mass, I slowly began to pay attention during the Eucharistic offering not to the priest's face at the altar or even his gestures. Not to the families gathered before me. But the large crucifix above the altar. As I learned to see the Eucharistic Prayer as a real encounter with Christ's sacrifice on the cross, I found myself better able to bear my sorrows. Christ, too, knows my darkness. He knows the limitations of what it means to be human. Yet, in the midst of his suffering, he did not stop loving. He transformed even death itself into a sacrifice of love. Was it not possible for me too to undergo this transformation? To leave my wounds on the altar, with those of Christ's, and to find myself transformed in love?

After an entire Lenten season of participating in Sunday Mass in this way, I found that I had been transformed by the language of sacrifice in the Eucharistic Prayer. Christ was presenting to me at every Mass the totality of love. He was giving me love in the midst of suffering, in the midst of sorrow. I could receive it. I could become it. I could, like Jesus, sacrifice my own infertility so that it may bear life in the world. I could adopt. I could foster. I could bear fruit through welcoming the orphan, the stranger, anyone in need.

In this sense, the language of sacrifice in the Roman Canon reminds us that the Mass is a sacrifice. It is a sacrifice of love. The more we receive this sacrifice, the more we offer this sacrifice of love ourselves, the more we can become God's love for the world. Total love is given in the Eucharist. Total love is received in the Eucharist.

The Structure of the Roman Canon

The Roman Canon is a highly structured prayer whose 2011 English translation has captured well the Latin style of the text. Traditionally, the Roman Canon is divided into the following parts, known by their Latin names (I have included the English translation after the Latin text)[29]:

1. Preface (with *Sanctus*, or "Holy, Holy")
2. *Te igitur* | "To you, therefore, most merciful Father"
3a. *In primis* | "which we offer you firstly"
3b. *Memento Domino famulorum* | "Remember Lord, your servants N. and N."
3c. *Communicantes* | "In communion with those whose memory we venerate."
4a. *Hanc igitur* | "Therefore, Lord, we pray...."
4b. *Quam oblationem* | "Be pleased, O God, we pray...."
5a. *Qui pridie* | "On the day before he was to suffer...."
5b. *Simili modo* | "In a similar way, when supper was ended...."
5c. *Mysterium fidei* | "The Mystery of Faith"
5d. *Unde et memores* | "Therefore, O Lord, / as we celebrate the memory...."
6a. *Supra quae* | "Be pleased to look upon these offerings"
6b. *Supplices te rogamus* | "In humble prayer we ask you, almighty God...."
7a. *Memento etiam* | "Remember also, Lord your servants N. and N.
7b. *Nobis quoque peccatoribus* | "To us, also, your servants, who though sinners...."
7c. *et societatem donare digneris* | "graciously grant some share / and fellowship"
8a. *Per quem haec omnia* | "through Christ our Lord."
8b. *Per ipsum et cum ipso* | "Through him, and with him, and in him."

Our families, our friends, our colleagues, all those on the margins: they need this love.

REPETITION IN THE ROMAN CANON

The Roman Canon repeats itself. It is never enough to refer simply to the sacrifice that is being offered. Bread and wine are gifts, sacrifices. Holy and unblemished sacrifices. The Church guards, unites, governs. We ask God to bless, acknowledge, and approve this offering. Christ takes up the chalice in his holy and venerable hands. We offer back to the Father Christ's Body and Blood as a pure victim, a holy victim, a spotless victim. If an English teacher happened upon the Roman Canon, she would have no problem making some edits for the sake of clarity.

But this is to misunderstand what is taking place in its repetitive speech. Repetition, of course, is the language of love. Having a son, I often find myself repeating the same songs and playing the exact same games for hours with our toddler. Happening upon my terribly written, angst-filled journal of my undergraduate days, I had no problem referring to the women whom I fell in love with as "beautiful and gorgeous," "intelligent and smart," "riveting and engaging." Language of repetition allows us to express the depths of our love, since no single word can capture our affections.

There is something like love's repetition going on in the Roman Canon. One word is not enough to refer to the gift of the Eucharist. One verb of offering is inadequate as we approach the throne of God, seeking to offer worship. We repeat ourselves again and again, because what do you do when you encounter Love itself?

Such repetition is really necessary for all of our prayer. Many people object to the Catholic Mass because it is so formulaic. Because we end up repeating ourselves, for the most part, from week to week. Can't we get a couple of new Eucharistic Prayers in there and change it up? Can't we redo the entire structure of the Mass for a change of pace?

The style of the Roman Canon actually invites us to appreciate the gift of repetition in prayer. This is hard for us. We constantly seek out the novel. We want what has never been said before. We want television that blows our minds because it pushes the boundaries of what we thought was possible. We don't want the same old, same old.

Yet it is repetition that actually forms habits in us. We go to the gym on Monday, on Tuesday, on Wednesday, and on and on. Eventually, by heading out to the gym at the same time, we develop a habit of exercise. We need it to be human. So too, the language of the Roman Canon develops in us a habit of sacrifice. We call this bread and wine a sacrifice, an offering, a solemn oblation. As we listen to this prayer, its form of speech ends up forming us. We begin to speak differently, to think about God differently. And we come back week after week, day after day, to engage in the same basic ritual form. Over a lifetime of repeating the Mass, we develop habits of sacrificial love.

THE SAINTS OF THE CANON

The first thing those new to the Roman Canon notice is the strange array of saints named in the midst of the prayer. Sure, we know some of them. Everyone knows Peter and Paul and probably many of the apostles. But who is Linus? Cosmas and Damian? Are these cartoon characters? Why are all these saints mentioned in the Roman Canon?

These saints are actually the key to unlocking the larger structure of the Roman Canon. Interpreters of the prayer have noticed that saints stand on both sides of the Roman Canon, almost like an altarpiece.[30] Before the Institution narrative, the Church brings to mind the Church on earth, including the Pope and other civil authorities, then recalls the heavenly Church with Mary the queen of saints, her spouse Joseph, the twelve apostles, and twelve early Christian martyrs. After the Institution narrative, the Church prays for the dead, that they may enjoy eternal life with God, and then remembers an additional group of martyr saints and virgins. Thus, in the recollection of the saints of the Roman Canon, you have the entire Church present. The living and the dead are bookended by the communion of saints.

In this way, the Roman Canon implicitly performs something that is said explicitly in other Eucharistic Prayers. The goal of the Eucharist is not simply making Christ present on earth. If that were the case, then we could speed through the prayer with ease. Rather, the Eucharist brings the Church together into one. It brings all of humanity together into one.

The presence of the communion of saints in the Roman Canon reminds every worshipper that Mass is not ultimately about my personal private experience of salvation. The Mass is about the renewal of all humanity, all the world, in love. We, gathered in that Church, are never alone. It is never simply our parish that has shown up. All the saints are present. All the angels. All the hosts of heaven. They're rooting for us to join their ranks, to move from the practice squad of the Mass to the choir of the heavenly saints.

When I go to Mass, it's never just about me. The Roman Canon testifies to this. It's about my vocation in the world to become a saint. A saint is not someone who is satisfied with his or her personal experience of God. The saints instead go forth, helping others to join their ranks. The Roman Canon is concerned about offering a sacrifice of love that increases the ranks of the saints. We never forget those who have died. Rather, we pray that they may become saints. We don't forget the living, hopeful that they might live as saints here and now. And we never forget the communion of saints, not because they are simply models for human behavior, but because they never forget us. As we pray every year on the feast of All Saints, during the prayer of the offerings of bread and wine:

> May these offerings we bring in honor of all
>   the Saints
> be pleasing to you, O Lord,
> and grant that, just as we believe the Saints
> to be already assured of immortality,
> so may we experience their concern for our
>   salvation.
> Through Christ our Lord.

I don't go to Mass for myself alone, but as someone who is learning what it means to join the choir of saints. I'm not here for a private experience of the joy that they now know. I go because my vocation is to encounter the love of Christ made present in the Eucharistic sacrifice and give it away prodigally. Foolishly. You know, like a saint.

> Lord Jesus Christ,
> as we gather together to celebrate your death and
>   resurrection,
> lead me to encounter the love that you have for
>   the Father,
> the love that you have for the human family.
> Transform me into this love through praying at
>   Mass.
> Let your Spirit inhabit me, so that I can become a
>   Eucharistic offering for the world.
> May I join the saints in their vocation to praise
>   God, inviting every man, every woman to share
>   in the joy of the Eucharistic kingdom.

QUESTIONS AND PRACTICES

1. The Roman Canon is a prayer that we have to learn to pray well. Find a copy of the prayer online and, based on what you've learned from this chapter, underline key phrases that you want to pay attention to the next time you pray the Canon at Mass.

2. We often understand sacrifice as something that is painful. But Christ's sacrifice on the cross, although painful, is also an act of supreme love. How has this understanding of sacrifice changed the way you think about the Mass? What would it mean to imitate this sacrifice in our daily lives?

3. The Eucharistic Prayer reveals our vocation as saints, meant to spread the Eucharistic love of the Mass to all the ends of the world. Do you think about this at Mass? If not, why not?

 CHAPTER EIGHTEEN

The Eucharistic Prayer

In this book we have explored a variety of prayers used in the Mass, including one of the Eucharistic Prayers: the Roman Canon. Most of us won't hear this prayer with any degree of regularity in our parishes (though perhaps, after the last chapter, you might wish you did). Still, the Roman Canon shares structural similarities with the other three Eucharistic Prayers that we pray at Mass. In this longer chapter, we will consider how to tune ourselves properly to pray these Eucharistic Prayers fruitfully. Once we know this structure, we will find it is easier to pay attention to what is happening at every Mass.

THE INTRODUCTORY DIALOGUE

The Eucharistic Prayer begins with an ancient dialogue of the Church. The priest says, "The Lord be with you," and we offer in return the greeting, "And with your spirit." Then the priest tells us, "Lift up your hearts." This, of course, doesn't mean that we are supposed to lift up our bodily hearts. The heart in the ancient world was the seat of one's affections, one's desires, one's very will. To lift up a heart, in this case, is to give over everything that we have to God. It is to leave behind, for a moment, the economy of the world and to enter instead into the grace of heaven.

Why, though, are we asked to leave behind the world when we have emphasized throughout this book that we are meant to bring everything about ourselves to Mass? Here, Blessed John Henry Newman might help us think about what it means to lift up our hearts to the Lord, to move from the earthly to the heavenly. In a sermon that he gave as an Anglican, Blessed John Henry Newman writes:

> Heaven then is not like this world: I will say what it is so much more like—*a church*. For in a place of public worship no language of this world is heard; there are no schemes brought forward for temporal objects, great or small; no information how to strengthen our worldly interests, extend our influence, or establish our credit. These things indeed may be right in their way, so that we do not set our hearts upon them; still (I repeat), it is certain that we hear nothing of them in a church. Here we hear solely and entirely of God. We praise Him, worship Him, sing to Him, thank Him, confess to Him, give ourselves up to Him, and ask His blessing. And therefore, a church is like heaven; viz. because both in the one and the other, there is one single sovereign subject—religion—brought before us.[31]

Throughout our week, we may grow accustomed to the speech of the world. We may find ourselves thinking more frequently about stocks and bonds than eternal life with God. We may practice not praise of God but hate of neighbor through words and deeds alike. We may gaze not on the living God but pornographic images of the flesh downloaded from the Internet. In the Eucharist, we will be asked to leave all this behind. We will be asked to give our memories, our desires, our understanding, our imaginations—everything about us—entirely over to God. When the priest exhorts us to "lift up your hearts," we must leave behind the language of the world to take up the salvific speech of heaven.

So we pray in return, "We lift them up to the Lord." We lift them up to the Lord because we know that God's vision is that of love. We lift them up to the Lord because we know that we need an encounter with the healing mercy of heaven so that we can offer the sacrifice of the Eucharist. We lift them up to the Lord because we want them to be reshaped by God so that a little piece of heaven might dwell on earth.

The dialogue continues with the priest inviting the Church to give thanks to the Lord. Our response is strange. "It is right and just." Imagine how weird it would be if someone proposed to you, and instead of saying, "Yes, I want to marry you with all of my heart," you'd say, "It is right and just."

"It is right and just" is a phrase that emerges from Roman court ceremonial. It is more like a pledge than a simple yes. I take you, Kara, to be my wife. "It is right and just." I promise to love you forever until the very end of our lives, to be with you even when you're on your deathbed, caring for you as my beloved. "It is right and just." I promise to lift up my heart, to let it be transformed, so that wherever I go it is on fire with the love of your own precious heart, Jesus. "It is right and just."

THE THANKSGIVING
"It Is Truly Right and Just"

Every Eucharistic Prayer in the Roman Catholic Mass begins with a Thanksgiving Preface, of which there are many options in the Roman Rite. In many ways, the preface has a format not unlike what we have already seen in the collect prayer. The priest continues the dialogue that had just ended. But now, rather than return the dialogue to us folks in the pews, the priest invites us to give thanks for something specific. The common preface for Eucharistic Prayer II states:

> It is truly right and just, our duty and our salvation,
> always and everywhere to give you thanks, Father
>   most holy,
> through your beloved Son, Jesus Christ,
> your Word through whom you made all things,
> whom you sent as our Savior and Redeemer,
> incarnate by the Holy Spirit and born of the Virgin.
>
> Fulfilling your will and gaining for you a holy people,
> he stretched out his hands as he endured his Passion,
> so as to break the bonds of death and manifest the
>   resurrection.
>
> And so with the Angels and all the Saints
> we declare your glory
> as with one voice we acclaim.

This Thanksgiving Preface, prayed during Ordinary Time, delights in what the Father has accomplished through the gift of his Son. The Word, which is the very meaning of creation, became flesh. God became one of us, sharing our flesh. He gave his will to the Father and, in the process, brought the Church into existence. The Holy People of God gather together to remember what has taken place through the Son. He died and rose again, and now the Church waits with longing for this good work to continue even in our own day.

While this is the most basic preface, the Church does change prefaces often during major liturgical seasons, on the feasts of saints, for the celebration of Masses for particular groups, and in the context of the sacraments. In this way, the prefaces give us a reason to celebrate the Eucharist. Most of the time, it's simply because Christ is wonderful. Because Christ has conquered death and given us this destiny too. But sometimes it's because before our eyes man and woman have become husband and wife, a living sign of Christ's love for the Church. Sometimes it's because we remember what Christ accomplished in the Incarnation, hoping that he'll come again to complete this work of love. Sometimes it's because our beloved friend, our spouse, our fellow student has fallen asleep in Christ, and we need to pray that he or she may join the Eucharistic chorus of praise in heaven.

As we can see, it's really important to pay attention to the prefaces of the Mass. If possible, purchase a personal Missal or download an app that will enable you to pray these prefaces at home before you come to the Eucharist. Then you will become practiced in contemplating the mysteries of salvation that the Church remembers at the Eucharistic liturgy.

THE *SANCTUS*
"Holy, Holy, Holy"

Like the Psalms, the *Sanctus* is not just a musical interlude. Instead, if you think about the Eucharistic Prayer
as an ascent to heaven, the *Sanctus* is an entry into the
heavenly worship of the angels—a joining together of the
voices of the Church on earth with heaven.

The text of the *Sanctus* consists of two biblical passages linked to one another. The first is from the Book
of Isaiah, where the prophet encounters the glory of the
Lord in the Temple. Isaiah hears the angelic host sing:

> "Holy, holy, holy is the LORD of hosts!" they
> cried one to the other. "All the earth is filled
> with his glory!" At the sound of that cry, the
> frame of the door shook and the house was
> filled with smoke.
>
> Then I [Isaiah] said, "Woe is me, I am
> doomed! For I am a man of unclean lips, liv-
> ing among a people of unclean lips, yet my
> eyes have seen the King, the LORD of hosts!"
> Then one of the seraphim flew to me, hold-
> ing an ember which he had taken with tongs
> from the altar. (Is 6:3–6)

Within the Old Testament, God's name is revealed
as holy, as sacred. To say the name of the Lord is to invoke
the Lord's presence. For this reason, the one who calls out
to God requires purification. The angelic hymn of praise
cannot be sung by us without preparation. Isaiah receives
a burning coal on his lips to purify his speech. For those
of us at Mass, everything we have done to this point has

been a preparation for the Eucharistic Prayer where we will call upon the name of the Lord.

The second Scriptural element of the *Sanctus* is taken from the Gospel of Matthew. As Jesus enters into Jerusalem and moves toward his passion, the crowds proclaim: "Hosanna to the Son of David; blessed is he who comes in the name of the Lord; hosanna in the highest" (Mt 21:9). This song offered by the crowd is an enthronement song, greeting the presence of the King of Israel. So too, the Church sings this praise as we enter into the Eucharistic Prayer. On the altar, the crucified and risen King will become present. He will invite us to eat his Body and drink his Blood, entering into the banquet of the kingdom of God.

The *Sanctus* is thus both a song of joy and a song to purify our hearts, to await the advent of God. It is a song of expectation, of desire, of longing. Our churches are the place where heaven and earth meet in cosmic joy.

We may struggle to see this in our parish church. After the Second Vatican Council, many parishes moved away from much of the art and architecture that had defined the Catholic imagination for centuries. Newly-built churches shunned stained glass windows of saints in favor of windows using geometric patterns of color more attuned to movements in modern art. Sparse spaces with little on the walls, no statues, no angelic hosts painted on the ceilings—some of these churches look more like gyms than the place where heaven and earth kiss.

The *Sanctus* testifies to a truth that we have forgotten. The Mass is not just our celebration, the gathering of this community here and now. It is always the liturgy of heaven and earth where God's glory is revealed. Even in the smallest parish church, with the most unremarkable sacred art, heaven and earth are wed. The song of the angels rings out. Our voices are joined with the voices of the heavenly liturgy. In the midst of this chorus of praise, the Lord Jesus Christ comes to join us.

Lest we think that the Mass is only about words, it is important to say something about the posture that we take in the Eucharistic Prayer. We move from standing among the angels to kneeling in prayer. The earliest Christians, as best as we can determine, would have prayed the Eucharistic Prayer standing up. In fact, Eastern Catholics pray the entire Divine Liturgy on Sundays standing. They don't kneel at all.

Kneeling, though, has been adopted as the Western posture to take during the Eucharistic Prayer from the moment of the *Sanctus* to the doxology (at least within the United States). Some have argued that kneeling is a penitential posture. While this was once true, the posture has a deeper meaning for those of us who practice it today. To kneel is to dispose our bodies toward an act of adoration. I don't simply pray with my mind, with the words that come out of my mouth. I pray with my body.

To kneel, then, is not to make ourselves miserable before God. It is simply to say that my body is ready to adore the king of the world. My body is given over to God.

THE EPICLESIS
Send Your Spirit

After the *Sanctus*, the Church moves toward the epiclesis, a calling down of the Holy Spirit on the gifts of bread and wine. In Eucharistic Prayer II, this calling down of the Holy Spirit provides rich food for the imagination: "You are indeed Holy, O Lord, the fount of all holiness. Make holy, therefore, these gifts, we pray, by sending down your Spirit upon them like the dewfall, so that they may become for us the Body and Blood of our Lord Jesus Christ."

The reference to dewfall is related to Israel being fed with manna in the desert. Israel complains to Moses in the desert that they have no food to eat. They say let's go back to Egypt, where at least we had stew. They doubt God's generosity to care for them. In the midst of this doubting, God offers bread from heaven, the food of the angels to sustain them. He only lets Israel take enough each day for their needs, forming them to trust in the Lord. Tomorrow, more will be given.

To ask for the Spirit to descend upon our gifts just like manna in the desert is to pray for God's generosity to become present once again. Let the bread of the angels that our forebears ate in the desert become present to us through this bread, through this wine. Let these gifts that we have brought become for us your gifts that bring us closer to you.

Yet, the image of dewfall should make us aware of something else. Think about early morning in the summer, when the earth has not yet succumbed to the suffocating humidity that we enjoy so often in the Midwest in July. When the grass, almost brown from lack of rain, nonetheless glistens with the dew that fell during the night. Dew seems to transform the created order, making it shimmer with beauty, making land that is dry become a place of refreshment.

The sequence (a hymn sung before the Gospel) for Pentecost Sunday employs this very same image for the Holy Spirit. In the English translation by Edward Caswall, we read:

> Heal our wounds, our strength renew;
> On our dryness pour Thy dew;
>> Wash the stains of guilt away:
>
> Bend the stubborn heart and will;
> Melt the frozen, warm the chill;
>> Guide the steps that go astray.

The author of this hymn knows that it's not only land that can be dry, that can be refreshed through the dew of the Spirit. Rather, we too become dry. Think, for a moment, about a knot that is so tight that it cannot be undone. By putting the knot in just a bit of water, the rope begins to loosen.

Every time we go to Mass, we pray that the dew of the Spirit might descend on us. Unloose my knotty tongue to praise you aright. Refresh my hardened heart, making it a place to delight in you, O Lord. The Holy Spirit, at every Mass, is not simply transforming bread and wine. The power of the Spirit is transforming the entire Christian people.

And it should be remembered that at the beginning of the Eucharistic Prayer, we pray for the Spirit. Everything that the Christian does unfolds in light of the Spirit of God. The power of the Holy Spirit gives us the desire to pray. The refreshing grace we experience in this prayer is the work of the Spirit. All of this is the delight of the

Spirit, renewing our wayward hearts to offer a sacrifice of praise to the triune God.

God is at work in our prayer. This should draw our attention to something important. After the Council, many noted that during Mass we should be called to full, conscious, and active participation. A bad understanding of this is that we should always be moving, always have a part, always be speaking. In fact, the participation that we are called to is deeper than this. We are called to make a space within ourselves for God to act among us. Sometimes we'll speak words. Sometimes we'll bring forth gifts. But we're called to this participation whether we're moving, speaking, or standing still.

Full, conscious, and active participation is not simply external. It is also an internal act, where we make ourselves ready for the Spirit to act among us.

THE INSTITUTION NARRATIVE AND CONSECRATION
"Do This in Memory of Me"

The grammar of the Eucharistic Prayer is really important. From the very beginning, the first person plural is used: we, our, us. Yet, as the prayer continues, there is a change in personal pronouns. The priest no longer speaks in the second personal plural (you) but takes up the words of Jesus, speaking about "my body" and "my blood."

The Institution narrative has been given pride of place in the Eucharistic Prayer. For what we remember at the Eucharist is Christ's self-giving love offered to us. We remember what Christ accomplished on the cross, his resurrection from the dead. We follow his instructions given on the night before he died: to make a Eucharistic or thanksgiving offering in memory of him.

But what do these words mean? What did Jesus give in offering to us his Body and his Blood? Joseph Ratzinger helps us to think about this question:

> The words of institution alone are not sufficient; the death alone is not sufficient; and even both together are still insufficient but have to be complemented by the Resurrection, in which God accepts this death and makes it the door into a new life. From out of this whole matrix—that he transforms his death, that irrational event, into an affirmation, into an act of love and of adoration—emerges his acceptance by God and the possibility of his being able to share himself in this way.
>
> On the Cross, Christ saw love through to the end. For all the differences there may be between the accounts in the various Gospels, there is one point in common: Jesus died praying, and in the abyss of death he upheld the First Commandment and held on to the presence of God. Out of such a death springs this sacrament, the Eucharist.[32]

The Institution narrative of the Eucharist does not simply recall the Last Supper. It is not simply inviting us to remember Jesus' death on the cross, where the Word made flesh took away all sins. Jesus Christ, who shares in our humanity, is truly and gloriously risen from the dead. He died the worst of deaths: alone, forsaken by friends, a seeming failure to his mission. Yet he loves even into the midst of death.

Out of this death, he is raised from the dead. Love wins! And love becomes present to us in Christ's Body and Blood, for us to share in the very love of God. We are invited to eat and drink the Eucharist, to die to ourselves, and to rise into the life of God. This is the order of love that Jesus Christ instituted.

When the priest speaks the words of the Institution narrative, he gives his voice over to Christ's "I." He stops speaking in his own person as representative of the Church and speaks entirely in the person of the Son. The person of the Son, who comes to give us a new covenant, sealed in his very blood, an image of his total self-giving love. At this moment, Christ becomes present to us. Not because Jesus was absent before. Remember, he is present to us in the Scriptures, in the singing assembly, in the ministry of the priest acting in the person of Christ.

He becomes present to us in his Body and his Blood because the words he spoke at the Last Supper promised that he would. These words promised that he would give the entirety of himself to us. He is totally present because Jesus Christ, if he is going to give himself to us, is going to give everything.

The Church refers to the transformation of bread and wine into Christ's Body and Blood as transubstantiation. The *Catechism of the Catholic Church* notes: "By the consecration the transubstantiation of the bread and wine into the Body and Blood of Christ is brought about. Under the consecrated species of bread and wine Christ himself, living and glorious, is present in a true, real, and substantial manner: his Body and his Blood, with his soul and his divinity (cf. Council of Trent: DS 1640; 1651)."[33]

Transubstantiation declares that Jesus is really and truly sacramentally present in the Eucharist. There's not half bread and part God. There's not partial wine and part of Jesus. Bread and wine cease functioning anymore as bread and wine. Their accidents or physical characteristics remain. But what the bread and wine really are is Christ's Body and Blood, his soul and his divinity. It's Jesus' very personal presence dwelling among us. He feeds us with what seems like bread, what seems like wine. But they're not. They are now Christ's personal presence dwelling and acting among us.

Of course, this does not mean that we will be able to see this presence. When microscopes first came into existence, there was a desire to observe the Eucharist under the microscope to discover if we might actually see Jesus' presence. That's not what happens in the sacrament. Christ's Body looks like bread. Christ's Blood looks like wine. And yet we adore the presence of the living God in our midst. It's St. Thomas Aquinas himself in his hymn *Tantum Ergo* who invites us to recognize the difficulty of seeing Jesus in the Eucharist:

> Down in adoration falling,
>> Lo! the sacred Host we hail;
> Lo! o'er ancient forms departing,
>> Newer rites of grace prevail;
> Faith for all defects supplying
>> Where the feeble senses fail.

At every Mass, we are called forth to see Christ present among us in his Body and Blood. We cannot see it as if we're conducting a scientific experiment. We see with the eyes of faith, with senses formed by adoration of the living God. In the Eucharist we practice the art of seeing—seeing beyond what is simply available to the senses and beholding the presence of the risen Lord, dwelling among us.

This practice of seeing with faith is necessary for the entire Christian life. As already noted, my wife and I have dealt with the pain of infertility. We have gazed with sorrow on our condition, wondering where God might be present there. Trained in Eucharistic seeing, to look past what is immediately visible, we were led to adopt. Now, out of what seemed like our death, has come new light. Going to Mass, practicing this kind of seeing, formed us to look beyond what seemed like pain and to see light shining forth in the darkness.

Transubstantiation isn't about magic. It's about a way of seeing.

MYSTERY OF FAITH
"We Proclaim Your Death, O Lord"

After the Institution narrative, the Church sings a response, what is described as the Mystery of Faith. Mystery is a funny word for us English-speakers. It doesn't just refer to a puzzle that might require work to solve. Rather, mystery is connected to God's plan hidden from the foundations of the world. What could not be seen has become seen. What could not be known has become known. All because God has revealed it to us in the person of his Son.

There are three options for this proclamation. The first proclaims, "We proclaim your Death, O Lord, and profess your Resurrection until you come again." The second, "When we eat this Bread and drink this Cup, we proclaim your Death, O Lord, until you come again." The last, "Save us, Savior of the world, for by your Cross and Resurrection you have set us free." Though different, they share three things in common.

First, these prayers are addressed to Jesus. Most of the Eucharistic Prayer seems to be addressed to the Father through the Son. But now, with Christ's Body and Blood having become present, we pray to Jesus himself. Already kneeling, we adore the Lord of the earth before us. Adoration is not something we do simply outside of Mass. Every time we approach the sacred elements, we are to adore the Lord. To sing to Jesus in the midst of the Eucharistic Prayer is to begin this act of adoration anew. To sing the mystery of faith is to prepare our hearts to adore the Lord in Holy Communion.

Second, each of the prayers puts Jesus' presence in the context of what he has done for humanity. Christ becomes present in the Eucharist not as a parlor trick. Jesus is the one who becomes present and raises death to new life. Jesus, whose death was the source of new life, is the one who transforms what it means to be human. To proclaim the mystery of faith is not to announce Jesus' presence as if he is some object. Rather, he is a person who has come to dwell among us, acting once again.

Third, we are not just remembering the activity of Jesus once upon a time. Jesus is going to act again here and now. His Death and Resurrection are relived when we eat the Body and Blood of Christ, when we proclaim to the world that Jesus is the living one who comes to free us from sin and death. Although it may not seem like it to us, the salvation of the world is being carried out every time we celebrate the Mass.

THE ANAMNESIS AND OBLATION
We Celebrate the Memorial, We Become the Offering

After a brief moment of communal singing, the priest begins to pray aloud again. This part of the Eucharistic Prayer is called the anamnesis or the "remembering." What do we remember? In Eucharistic Prayer IV, we hear:

> Therefore, O Lord,
> as we now celebrate the memorial of our redemp-
>   tion,
> we remember Christ's Death
> and his descent to the realm of the dead,
> we proclaim his Resurrection
> and his Ascension to your right hand,
> and, as we await his coming in glory,
> we offer you his Body and Blood,
> the sacrifice acceptable to you
> which brings salvation to the whole world.

If you're like me, you may begin to wonder if the Eucharistic Prayer just really needed an editor. Didn't we already remember the redemption? What have we been doing all along?

But this remembering is different. With Christ's Body and Blood present among us, we remember what Christ did because now we are dedicating ourselves to making the very same offering. The whole Church is to make this offering in light of Christ, to give ourselves over to the Eucharistic love of the Son.

The Church continues in Eucharistic Prayer IV:

> Look, O Lord, upon the Sacrifice
> which you have provided for your Church,
> and grant in your loving kindness
> to all who partake of this one Bread and one
> Chalice
> that, gathered into one body by the Holy Spirit,
> they may truly become a living sacrifice in Christ
> to the praise of your glory.

The Church on earth has a vocation. She is to become a Eucharistic offering for the world. In fact, at every Mass it is the Church herself who is offered in the Eucharist.

This is not a revolutionary theology, introduced only after the Second Vatican Council. It's present in the words of Augustine of Hippo himself, preaching to those Christians recently baptized into the Church in Hippo at Pentecost. He exhorts his assembly:

> So if you want to understand the body of Christ, listen to the apostle telling the faithful, You, though, are the body of Christ and its members (1 Cor 12:27). So if it's you that are the body of Christ and its members, it's the mystery meaning you that has been placed on the Lord's table; what you receive is the mystery that means you. It is to what you are that you reply Amen, and by so replying you express your assent. What you hear, you see, is the Body of Christ, and you answer, Amen.

So be a member of the body of Christ, in order to make that Amen true.[34]

Although Augustine is speaking about receiving communion, his words are essential to figuring out what happens in the anamnesis, or offering. Christ is present among us. His self-giving love is present among us. And now, we offer Christ's love back to the Father. We offer this love not by resacrificing Christ on the cross again and again. We offer this love not because God needs it. We offer it because we are called to offer ourselves in love in light of what the Son has revealed.

Our deepest identity as the Church is not a gathering of like-minded, friendly folk who happen to all enjoy the same music or be around the same age or share the same political party. Rather, the Church is Christ's Body given to the world. We remember this offering, and in the act of remembering, we become this offering again. We become God's self-sacrificial love for the world.

That means that we actually have to love one another and to love the world. We have to become like Jesus, to shape our lives according to the self-giving love of the Son. How do we do this?

Of course, in the Eucharistic Prayer it is not we who are doing this work but the Holy Spirit. That being said, the Spirit cannot work unless we give some part of ourselves over to the Spirit. We have to have the material for the Spirit to work on. Here, we become proper matter for this sacrifice of love when we actually love all people in the world. When we practice love within the life of the Church.

It is often said by well-intentioned Millennials that they don't need a Church to worship God. They're right.

You don't need a Church to worship if you mean to have a private experience of God's presence, to thank God, even to love God. You need a Church because you're not just supposed to love Jesus, but to become Jesus' love for the world. The Church is that place where we enter into this school of love. At every Eucharistic liturgy, we receive total love. We are to become this love, this unity, for the entire world.

After all, in the Gospel of John, after they have eaten the Last Supper, Jesus bends down and washes the feet of his disciples. Then he speaks to them, explaining what he has done: "If I, therefore, the master and teacher, have washed your feet, you ought to wash one another's feet. I have given you a model to follow, so that as I have done for you, you should also do" (Jn 13:14–15). On Holy Thursday, after the priest has performed this rite of the foot-washing, we are to sing the following chant (*"Ubi Caritas"*) as stipulated by the Roman Missal:

> By the love of Christ we have been brought together:
> let us find in him our gladness and our pleasure;
> may we love him and revere him, God the living,
> and in love respect each other with sincere hearts.

> So when we as one are gathered all together,
> let us strive to keep our minds free of division;
> may there be an end to malice, strife and quarrels,
> and let Christ our God be dwelling here among us.

The Church, in this sense, is only possible because of the love of God received on the cross. The Church is becoming ever more and more this love for the world. Christ becomes present to feed us, the Church. When we feed on his Body and Blood, even as we are praying this Eucharistic Prayer, we ask God to make the Church what she is always supposed to be: a sacrifice of love.

Ultimately, this is Pope Francis's concern about evangelization. The parish isn't supposed to be about itself. It's not supposed to be about the artificial regulations that the parish creates for baptism, for first communion, even for confirmation. It's not supposed to be about committees of like-minded folks planning carnivals. It's about a Church moving out from the Eucharistic love of God, becoming this very same sacrifice for the world.

THE INTERCESSION
For the Living and the Dead

Having become this sacrifice of love on the altar, the Church assumes her vocation as one who prays. We pray for the Church, for the Pope, the bishop, and all clergy. We pray for all those who have died. We pray for all the dead that they might live in union with the Blessed Virgin Mary, with St. Joseph, with the Apostles, and all the Saints.

Again, if you think the Eucharistic Prayer is about escaping the world, then the intercessions in the midst of this prayer don't make sense. In fact, it is because the Church has assumed her vocation as a sacrifice of love for the world that we can pray for the world.

Yet these prayers are not simply directed to God on behalf of the world. In fact, they are connected fundamentally to the union of the Church. We are praying that the Church might become the communion of love that we hope for. There is a concreteness to this communion.

The Pope isn't just a random leader. He is the sign of unity and love among Christians. The local bishop isn't just a guy that we like or dislike. He serves as a living sign of the Church's presence in this area of the world. Thus, at every Eucharistic liturgy we pray that the Church on earth might become what she is supposed to be: a communion of love, of peace, and of unity that renews the human race.

In this communion, the dead aren't the forgotten. Most of us will be forgotten by the world. Sure, our families will remember us for a generation or two after we die. Then we will only resurface in family history projects that our future great-great-great grandchildren will perform. But in the Church, we don't forget anyone. The communion of love that we share with the dead, with the saints, it crosses the boundaries of time and space.

The Church is such a powerful union of love that we can pray for the dead. We remember them to God, for they are still part of us.

Intercessory prayer is not ultimately about trying to convince God to change his mind. It's actually about a communion of love. Every evening at our home, during night prayer, my family prays for the sick, for our priests, for my son's teachers, for everyone who has asked for our prayers. This is more than a pious act of faith. It is a real remembering of the needs of the world before God. It is a communion of love, where the concerns of others become mine.

We can build this communion of love in concrete ways, beyond offering a quick prayer for a friend. We can fast for the healing of a sick person in our life. We can go to Mass and offer it up for the needs of a coworker. These are real acts of love, which help bring unity to all the world, the unity that Christ first intended for the human family.

This is the vocation of the Church in the world: to bring this unity to everyone.

THE DOXOLOGY

At the conclusion of the Eucharistic Prayer, the Church prays the doxology: "Through him, and with him, and in him, O God, almighty Father, in the unity of the Holy Spirit, all glory and honor is yours, for ever and ever." We then sing forth, "Amen."

This doxology, at the conclusion of the prayer, shows us that the unity that we want to build among the human family is actually the unity of God. God the Father, who is the source of all love. God the Son, who is love made flesh, dwelling among us, teaching us to offer this same act of love back to the Father as children of God. God the Spirit, who is the very possibility of this return gift of love; the God who woos us in the interior of our hearts to love God anew.

In some ways, the doxology serves as a corrective to the modern religious imagination. Religion is not a personal project of building ourselves up. We are not the sole creators of human unity, because every notion we have of unity is inadequate compared to God. Every sense we have of what love means is corrected by the God who is love.

The Eucharistic Prayer invites us into the school of love. To learn precisely what love is by entering into the very life of the Trinity. To learn to practice love in singing hymns of praise to the living God, hymns of praise that bring us together into a sacrifice of love.

Amen, let us become one with this God.

Let us eat Christ's Body and drink his Blood.

And through this eating, this drinking, this
   adoration, this transformation of your Church,
   change the world.

Change the world so that every part of it is a
   living sign of your love, your unity. Until, one
   day, the whole world will be lifted up and
   become forever and ever and ever a liturgy
   of praise to you. Amen. Amen indeed.

QUESTIONS AND PRACTICES

1. Obtain a copy of one of the Eucharistic Prayers. Spend a couple of minutes each day meditating on it.

2. Many avoid going to Mass, saying that they don't need the Church to worship God. Perhaps you're one of them. After reading this chapter, how might you respond to such a person? How does the Eucharistic Prayer offer another approach to worship in which the Church is necessary?

3. This chapter suggests a variety of practices to help you pray the Eucharistic Prayer better. What practices are you attracted to? What other practices might you use to pray each part of the prayer better?

4. How does your church's music and architectural space prepare you to enter into the heavenly liturgy? What might you do within this space to make this aspect of the Eucharistic Prayer more evident?

CHAPTER NINETEEN

The Communion Rite

O Sacred Banquet

When we brought our newborn son home from the hospital, a legion of coworkers volunteered to bring meals to our house. Later in the evening, after our son had gone down for his four-hour nap, we joyfully feasted on the meal brought by friends. We drank a bit of wine to unwind. We spoke about our day, about the gift of love that our son was to us.

As time has passed, meals around our table have ceased being quite so contemplative. The toddler now eats his food with speed, absentmindedly throwing broccoli across the room. He cries out, expressing his lack of manners, "More!" And we discern what he actually wants from the array of choices on the table. More bread? More water? That knife in the middle of the table that we have hidden from you? My wife and I try to catch up with one another at the same time that the toddler son wants us to regale him with a catalogue of songs that he finds fitting for meal time. We rush away from the table to clean dishes before bath time commences.

Yet at every meal, from the contemplative ones of infancy to the harried dinners of later toddlerhood, there is something sacred about mealtime in our home.

It serves as a transition from the busyness of our work, of our domestic tasks, to the peace of evening. It is generally followed by the reading of books, by leisurely conversations, and eventually the peaceful rest of sleep.

At Mass, there is also a mealtime. This mealtime, of course, is not separate from the sacrifice of the Mass. Having listened to the Scriptures and having prayed the Eucharistic Prayer, we are invited now to the Supper of the Lamb. There we will receive the living God who is the source of our rest. We will sup at the altar of God, who makes all things new. The act of eating and drinking that we perform at Mass is our participation in the sacred banquet of the kingdom of God. Therefore, there are rites that precede the eating and drinking, rites that prepare us to savor our communion with Jesus Christ and one another.

THE LORD'S PRAYER

I regularly interview undergraduates on campus for programs housed in the McGrath Institute for Church Life at Notre Dame. I always ask about their prayer lives. Inevitably, they tell a similar story. Growing up, they didn't really have a life of prayer. All they had was the *Our Father*, given to them by their parents. When they grew up, they went to some youth ministry gathering or retreat where they learned how to really pray to God, using their own words, not rote prayers. Finally, they had made their faith their own and could talk to God using any old speech. They now looked dismissively at the *Our Father* as an inauthentic way of praying.

This approach to prayer favored by some youth ministries does a big disservice to our students. The Lord's

Prayer isn't just some prayer to be learned by heart and then mechanically prayed. At every Mass, right before we receive the Eucharist, we stand, and the priest says, "At the Savior's command and formed by divine teaching, we dare to say...." If the Lord's Prayer consisted simply of boring old words, then why all this hubbub about praying it? *We dare to say?* I mean, I say the prayer all the time. I pray it with my son in the evening. I pray it when I encounter a car accident on the side of the road. I pray it all day long.

In fact, at Mass we learn precisely how revolutionary the Lord's Prayer is. Sure it can be prayed in a way that is totally uncommitted, totally apathetic. But all prayers can be offered in this way. What makes the Lord's Prayer particularly important, especially in the Mass, is that it prepares us to approach the banquet of the Lord, to receive our daily bread.

It's no accident that we pray the *Our Father* just as we approach communion. The Christian, after all, is the one who has received the gift of being able to address God as Father. We address God as Father not because God is male or female, but because he is the Father of the Son, Jesus Christ. In baptism, we have entered into the place of the Son. We have become children of the Father. The confidence, the intimacy, shared between Jesus and the Father is the intimacy that we should have with God. A professor of mine, Fr. John Dunne, C.S.C., often said that Christian prayer is jumping into Jesus. Praying the Lord's Prayer, we jump into the sonship of the risen Lord. It becomes ours. We don't just pray the words that Jesus taught us. We let our speech become the speech of Jesus.

We also note in this prayer that the God we pray to is in heaven. We may think about this as a description of God's remoteness from us, but at Mass, we are preparing to enter into the heavenly banquet, to dine at heaven's table. In the Book of Isaiah, the heavenly banquet of the Lord is described: "On this mountain the LORD of hosts / will provide for all peoples / A feast of rich food and choice wines, juicy, rich food and pure, choice wines" (Is 25:6). The God who is serving this heavenly banquet, who is offering to us at Mass his Body and Blood, is not remote. He is holy. God's name is hallowed. But he is not distant. The "heavenly" nature of God means something else.

What makes the banquet heavenly is that it is not for the rich alone. It's not for the powerful alone. It's for all who come with empty hearts and hands to feed at God's sacrificial table. Hallowed, indeed, is the name of Jesus, who comes to establish the kingdom's banquet. Who establishes the Eucharistic reign of God on earth, even now, at this Mass. Who brings God's mercy to all the corners of the world.

Yet there's something for us to do. God establishes the heavenly reign in Christ. We have to give our wills over to this reign: *thy kingdom come, thy will be done.* It's no easy thing to let God's kingdom come. The first sin of Adam and Eve is a refusal to give their wills to God; that is, to say *thy will be done.* After all, many of us think, it's *my* will that's best. My will for my life. My will for your life. My will for the world. God's kingdom begins to reign on earth when we give our wills over to the Father.

Isn't this what Jesus does in the Garden of Gethsemane: "Father, if you are willing, take this cup away from me; still, not my will but yours be done" (Lk 22:42). Jesus is not saying, "Well, whatever you want, Dad." He is living in total trust that through his death and resurrection, the foliage of the kingdom of God will sprout in the hearts of women and men.

As we approach the altar, we remind ourselves that the reign of God enacted by Jesus is not that of the powerful, those who can have their will be done. It is the peaceable kingdom of those who offer their wills in love to the Father. Let it be done, Lord, on earth as it is in heaven. Let heaven reign here and now.

Of course, it is the kingdom that is still coming into existence. The Mass is not heaven on earth per se. After all, there is still a distance between God's reign of peace and our own world. The Lord's Prayer is, therefore, an "eschatological prayer," one that looks to God's final establishment of the reign of peace in the world. This "eschatological" orientation is appropriate to the Mass in particular. It is a common practice in some parishes to hold hands during the Lord's Prayer at Mass. While this is a beautiful image of community, there is an inadequacy to it. The kingdom of God is present not just among those of us gathered in this church. God's kingdom is in-breaking, it's interrupting our complacency, our little circle of friends who love one another.

The Mass is also this in-breaking of the kingdom of God into the midst of the Church. Recently, some liturgical theologians have argued for the wisdom of the entire assembly, including the priest, facing toward the east during the Eucharistic Prayer. The priest would pray not facing the people but in the very same direction that the people of God also pray.

The east is the direction of the rising sun. To look toward the east is to embrace the cosmic symbol of the sun, to turn with hope that Christ's kingdom might come here and now. The Church that prays at Mass is not the select gathering of the redeemed, who can now turn inward to contemplate themselves. Rather, this is the Church still longing for the coming of the kingdom. Priest and people alike, awaiting the resurrected Lord.

Of course, we don't need to turn to the east to take up this disposition, even if it might be a good bodily posture to sometimes adopt at Mass. As Cardinal Ratzinger suggested, we can turn toward the crucifix in this prayer. For on the cross, we see the coming kingship of God revealed in the powerlessness of love. The important thing during the Lord's Prayer is that we don't turn inward. This isn't a special prayer for just us. It's a prayer that makes possible the coming of the kingdom of God.

In the Lord's Prayer, we then ask for our daily bread. Early Christians didn't understand this request as a desire merely to be fed every day, even though that is a good desire to have. The Greek word for daily in the Lord's Prayer is *epiousios*, which means more than just a daily meal. It means the bread that is appropriate for what one needs this particular day. Here, bread is a metaphor for all of our nourishment. It's for food and love alike.

When the Bible was translated into Latin, Jerome read *epiousios* as "supersubstantial" in Latin (*supersubstantialem*). This word also means what is needed for the sustaining of life. But it takes on the character of a Eucharistic request. Give us the bread that is supersubstantial. The bread from heaven, the Eucharistic bread that feeds our greatest desires. At every Mass, God has answered this prayer. He comes to feed us with the finest wheat.

We also pray again for forgiveness: *Forgive us our trespasses, as we forgive those who trespass against us.* Jesus frequently ate with people he shouldn't have been eating with. In the midst of these meals, he invites sinners and tax collectors, Pharisees and Scribes, toward forgiveness. This forgiveness from God to all people is part of the coming kingdom. At every Mass, the Lord sits down at table with us, sinner and saint alike, to forgive us of our trespasses, if we only ask. We are like the prodigal Son coming homeward, discovering there the Father awaiting our arrival, running toward us, preparing to hold a party for us sinners. As N. T. Wright writes:

> The Eucharist is the direct historical descendant, not just of the Last Supper, but of those happy and shocking parties which Jesus shared with all and sundry as a sign that they were surprisingly and dramatically forgiven. This meal, in other words, is linked directly to the meals which Jesus explained by telling the story of the Running Father. Hold that image in your mind as you come to Communion. Whichever far country you may be in, and for whatever reason, you don't have to stay there one moment longer. By the time you get to the words "forgive us our trespasses," you will already have been embraced by the Father who has run down the road to meet you.[35]

If we want to be part of this party, we only need to ask. We only need to offer this forgiveness to our brothers and sisters along the way. The coming of this forgiveness, of this divine mercy made present in the Church, is the arrival of the kingdom of God.

Lastly, we ask God to keep us from temptation, away from evil, away from the Evil One. The coming of God's reign can be delayed through human sin. We can create disunity and discord, destroying communion. Sin is real, and the Lord's Prayer notes that the devil is real. As we approach the Eucharist at Mass, we ask that God will rescue us from our temptations, from the work of the Evil One in the Church, in the world, in our own lives.

The final part of the Lord's Prayer is the doxology, added on at the Second Vatican Council. The priest takes up our last common petition that we might be rescued from evil, from the Evil One. We sing out, "For the kingdom, the power and the glory are yours now and for ever." God's kingdom will defeat sin and death. God's power is the ultimate power. God's glory is even now present among us. The kingship of Jesus, the glorious ruler of heaven and earth, is to be the kingship of the Church gathered at Mass. Let it be this now, let it be this forever. As we eat and drink the Body and Blood of Christ, we are citizens of *this* kingdom. Our citizenship is in the city of God.

So, the Lord's Prayer is no rote prayer. Each time we pray it, whether in Mass or not, God's reign begins once again, and we renew our promise to let God's will be done. Here and now and forever and ever.

THE RITE OF PEACE
"Peace I Leave You, My Peace I Give You"

During our dorm Masses at Notre Dame, the sign of peace can last a long time and take a variety of forms. There is the bro-hug: one arm around the neck, the other giving a slightly violent tap to the back. This hug seems to say, "Peace to you, but still—watch out." Then there is the catch-up sign of peace. Here, I don't simply offer Christ's peace to you but also talk to you about the weekend, the parties we attended, and the tests coming up.

Whatever the style of hug, a Notre Dame sign of peace reveals a problem many Catholics have with our understanding of this rite. As human beings in the modern world, we long for a community that we don't possess. So many of us live far away from our extended families. We live in cities where we are seemingly unknown. We might be able to Skype with friends and family on a regular basis, but this communication (no matter how excellent) still leaves us longing for human touch—a hug or handshake that says, "It will be alright."

These are concerns that the Church must deal with. We need communities of love that care for one another. We need parishes that regularly visit the elderly, those who might go weeks without a visitor. We need young adult groups where the loneliness of a new city can be soothed through developing friendships. The parish should become a place where Christ's peace is available to all.

But the sign of peace at Mass is not this moment. The sign of peace finds its root in Jesus' exhortation to forgive one's enemy before coming to the altar: "If you bring your gift to the altar, and there recall that your brother has anything against you, leave your gift there at the altar, go first and be reconciled with your brother, and then come and offer your gift" (Mt 5:23–24). In the Divine Liturgy of Eastern Catholicism, the sign of peace actually takes place before the Eucharistic Prayer because it is a moment of self-examination. Am I ready to come to the altar of God? Have I loved my neighbor well? Is there anger between us?

At the sign of peace, we are invited through an encounter with our Mass-neighbor to examine ourselves once again for any sin that we might have before we receive the living God. Sometimes this is pretty easy. When I'm at Mass, sitting next to my sibling who threw a truck at my head, I should forgive him. When I'm at Mass, sitting next to my spouse and annoyed that she doesn't clean up after herself (this is hypothetical), I should forgive her. I should also ask myself if I need forgiveness.

This forgiveness is to be offered in the Eucharist. As the priest prays, "Lord Jesus Christ, / who said to your Apostles: / Peace I leave you, my peace I give you, / look not on our sins, / but on the faith of your Church, / and graciously grant her peace and unity / in accordance with your will." We do sin. We do have enmity that keeps us apart.

Before coming to Communion, we are asked to frankly acknowledge our failures to love. We are to trust that the faith of the Church, the faith of the communion of saints, can be healing for us. We are asked to pray for God's peace to dwell among us, even now. To heal those wounds that keep us from loving God and neighbor aright. To bring us closer to the beatific vision, where we see God face-to-face and join the communion of saints in their Eucharistic hymn of praise.

THE FRACTION OF THE BREAD
"Behold the Lamb of God"

In this book we've already addressed one famous altar-piece, the Isenheim. But there is another we can meditate on as we approach Communion: the Ghent altarpiece, by Van Eyck, from 1432. In this masterpiece, soldiers, peasants, merchants, monks and hermits, and the entire communion of saints make their way in the midst of a city toward an altar. On this altar, surrounded by angels with incense and saints in song, is the slain Lamb. From the wound of the Lamb, a chalice is being filled with blood. Above the Lamb is the Spirit of the Lord, illuminating the entire scene. We are in the midst of the new heaven and earth spoken of in the Book of Revelation.

We at Mass enter into this scene. Like the heavenly Jerusalem, we cry aloud singing, "Lamb of God, you take away the sins of the world, have mercy on us … grant us peace." All the while, the priest breaks the Host into pieces for the distribution of Communion. But the priest is also doing something else. The bread that is broken on the altar is Christ's Body. We know that the Body of Christ was broken on the cross. It is from the wounds of our Lord that our salvation is to come forth. It is in the midst of a broken world that the Lamb of God makes himself known. So too, as we sing this chant and gaze on the broken Body of Christ, we are invited to consider the redemption that Christ promises for a broken world, for my broken world.

Here, I think especially of my students who suffer so much from anxiety. They want lives in which there is no failure. They only want to know success and happiness. And when failure strikes, when wounds happen, they can't take it. Yet if God makes his presence known among us through broken bread, is it not possible that the brokenness of our lives is also the place where the Lamb of God is to be found? *Lamb of God, you take away the sins of the world, have mercy on us. Grant us peace.*

After praying for a fruitful communion by the assembly, the priest then invokes us to adore the Lamb of God: "Behold the Lamb of God, behold him who takes away the sins of the world. Blessed are those called to the supper of the Lamb." This invitation to "behold" contains much imagery for reflection. Of course, we know that this is a quotation from the Gospels. After Jesus has been baptized, after he has thrown his lot in with sinful Israel and thus all of humanity, he approaches John the Baptist and John cries out, "Behold, the Lamb of God, who takes away the sin of the world" (Jn 1:29). Now, we stand before the Eucharistic presence of Christ, beholding this Lamb. We behold the one who comes to liberate us from sin and death, enacting God's kingdom of peace and justice.

"Beholding" is an important word. To behold is not simply to look at something for a bit, to give it a cursory glance and then to move on. To behold something is to love it, to contemplate it, to give ourselves over to enjoying it. In this sense, the priest's invitation is a perfect description of the entire Christian life. We are to learn to behold the Lamb of God through this moment of Eucharistic encounter. In the process of our beholding, of our loving, of our savoring, we will hear the following cry from the slain Lamb, "Behold, I make all things new" (Rev 21:5).

We then cry out, "Lord, I am not worthy that you should enter under my roof, but only say the word and my soul shall be healed." The text is taken from the Gospel of Matthew. The centurion whose servant is at home, paralyzed, asks Jesus to heal the servant. Jesus says he's on his way. But the centurion cries out, "Lord, I am not worthy to have you enter under my roof; only say the word and my servant will be healed" (Mt 8:8). The text is changed just a bit. We ask for the healing of our soul. Does this mean that our body is left out?

Of course not! After all, it's the Lamb that was slain, the Body of Christ broken and wounded, that is the source of our healing. The soul is simply a part that stands for the whole. The soul is our life-force, our breath, our living vitality. Christ will enter into our bodies in Communion, transforming this soul. Are we ever worthy to receive this grace? this healing? this gift? Christ will heal us. He will make us worthy. He will invite us to the Supper of the Lamb, feeding us as infants not yet ready to sup on their own.

The poet George Herbert describes the proper attitude that we should have as we join the Eucharistic banquet. He writes:

> Love bade me welcome: yet my soul drew back,
> > Guilty of dust and sin.
> But quick-eyed Love, observing me grow slack
> > From my first entrance in,
> Drew nearer to me, sweetly questioning,
> > If I lacked anything.

"A guest," I answered, "worthy to be here":
      Love said, "You shall be he."
"I the unkind, the ungrateful? Ah my dear,
      I cannot look on thee."
Love took my hand, and smiling did reply,
      "Who made the eyes but I?"

"Truth Lord, but I have marred them: let my shame
      Go where it doth deserve."
"And know you not," says Love, "who bore the
      blame?"
      "My dear, then I will serve."
"You must sit down," says Love, "and taste my meat":
      So I did sit and eat.[36]

The Lamb of God will make us worthy. The Lamb of God himself, both the Host and the food, will prepare a place in our heart to welcome the living God. I am not worthy to receive you. I have not loved well. I am a sinner. But Love itself bade me welcome to the Supper of the Lamb.

COMMUNION
"Learn to Savor How Good the Lord Is" (Ps 34:9)

Quiet now descends upon our parish church as we approach Christ's Body and Blood. Perhaps we kneel for a bit, praying that Christ will create a space in our hearts to receive the living God, that we will learn to be the blessed spouse of the Bridegroom. We should take our time here.

Parishes often fail at this moment most of all. We rush ahead, trying to get everyone fed as quickly as possible. Here's the Body. Here's the Blood. Let's get going.

But the moment of Communion is an occasion for personal encounter with the living God. Our postures represent this encounter. Some receive the Body of Christ in their hands. A certain group of liturgical theologians blame this posture for creating a lack of Eucharistic devotion, but that's silly. After all, it's Cyril of Jerusalem who notes that this posture is in fact appropriate for receiving the king of heaven and earth:

> So when you come forward, do not come with arm extended or fingers parted. Make your left hand a throne for your right, since your right hand is about to welcome a king. Cup your palm and receive in it Christ's body, saying in response *Amen*.... After partaking of Christ's body, go to receive the chalice of his blood. Do not stretch your hands for it. Bow your head and say *Amen* to show your homage and reverence, and sanctify yourself by partaking also of Christ's blood.[37]

When we receive Christ's Body in our hands, we should tenderly place it into our mouths. We should drink lovingly from the cup, adoring Christ. We may close our eyes as we do this, receiving the very presence of Love dwelling among us.

Others will receive the Body of Christ directly on the tongue. This posture, too, is very appropriate. Often when my toddler son is in the midst of playing, he'll run up to me and open his mouth to receive a snack. So too, we come forward to God as children waiting to be fed from the hand of our beloved parent. Some will receive in churches where they kneel at an altar rail. In every case, the important point is to receive Christ's Body and Blood in prayer.

The Church has chosen Communion Antiphons— short passages from Scripture—to savor as we eat and drink the Body and Blood of Christ. For example, at Pentecost we hear, "They were all filled with the Holy Spirit and spoke of the marvels of God, alleluia" (Acts 2: 4, 11). On the Twelfth Sunday in Ordinary Time, "The eyes of all look to you, LORD, and you give them their food in due season" (Ps 145:15).

Many parishes, however, do not sing or chant these antiphons, choosing instead to sing hymns that take up the themes of the antiphon, allowing us to "Learn to savor how good the LORD is; / happy are those who take refuge in him" (Ps 34:9).

The period after Communion should be a time of silent meditation, perhaps facilitated by a Communion motet or choral anthem. Many parishes, unfortunately, seem uncomfortable with the silence that should follow the reception of Communion, filling every moment with a hymn. If we run out of verses, start again. If we finish this hymn, sing another. The Communion Antiphon is not about covering this action. It's about meditation, an occasion to pray.

Our prayer after Communion is a time for us to express Eucharistic love to the Lord of heaven and earth. The poet Christina Rossetti, in "After Communion," gives us some images that we might consider as a post-Communion thanksgiving:

> Why should I call Thee Lord, Who art my God?
> Why should I call Thee Friend, Who art my
>   Love?

Or King, Who art my very Spouse above?
Or call Thy Spectre on my heart Thy rod?
  Lo, now Thy banner over me is love,
All heaven flies open to me at Thy nod:
For Thou hast lit Thy flame in me a clod,
  Made me a nest for dwelling of Thy Dove.
  What wilt Thou call me in our home above,
Who now hast called me friend? how will it be
  When Thou for good wine settest forth the
    best?
Now Thou dost bid me come and sup with Thee,
  Now Thou dost make me lean upon Thy
    breast:
How will it be with me in time of love?[38]

Throughout the Mass, we have called God by name. At Communion, there is no longer any distance between us and the living God. We are united as Spouses at least for a moment. The Holy Spirit, through the Eucharist, dwells in our hearts. We have renewed our spousal commitments, our spousal love to God.

In fact, every time we adore the Eucharist outside of Mass, this is what we're doing. We're longing for that total union with God that is our promise when earth passes away and heaven comes to dwell among us. We need time and space both after Communion and during the rest of our lives to adore the Eucharist. To love the Christ, who first loved us.

The Mass is not just any meal. It's not just any supper. It's the wedding banquet of the Lamb where heaven and earth are wed. Where heaven and earth are wed on my very lips, when I receive Christ's Body and Blood. This experience is reserved not simply for mystics and hermits; it is the mystical, sacramental life given to every Catholic during the Eucharist. Indeed, every Communion is a chance for us to taste and see the goodness of the Lord, and to offer in return a heart wounded by Love.

This silence after Communion is interrupted only by the words of the priest who now invites us to stand. More silence is offered to God, and the Prayer after Communion is offered. These prayers move us to give thanks for what God has done in giving us his Body and his Blood. On the Thirtieth Sunday in Ordinary Time, we pray:

> May your Sacraments, O Lord, we pray,
> perfect in us what lies within them,
> that what we now celebrate in signs
> we may one day possess in truth.
> Through Christ our Lord.

In almost every one of these prayers, there is a sense that the Eucharist itself is still just a foretaste of what is to come. Some youth groups used to say something like, "The Mass Never Ends…." They were wrong. The Mass will end. The sacrament of Christ's Body and Blood, no matter how wondrous, will end, and we will no longer feast on Christ's Body and Blood through signs. Instead, we will savor being in the presence of the living God, joining the communion of saints, singing aloud a hymn of praise for all heaven to hear. This Eucharist of heaven, this Mass of eternal life, will never end. It is the very Mass that we are prepared to participate in by heading to our local parish every Sunday and discovering there a foretaste of what is to come:

O Sacrament, most Holy,
O Sacrament Divine,
All praise and all thanksgiving,
  Be every moment Thine.

QUESTIONS AND PRACTICES

1. What new insights have you taken from this chapter that will help you prepare yourself to receive Communion? How do the Communion Rites dispose you for fruitful reception of Christ's Body and Blood?

2. The Communion Rites should leave ample time for silence. Does your parish observe this silence? If so, how? If not, why not?

3. Write your own prayer or poem to recite after receiving the Eucharist. Pray it each day.

4. Spend thirty minutes in Eucharistic Adoration every week for half a year. How has this prayer before the Eucharist changed how you receive the Body and Blood of Christ?

CHAPTER TWENTY

Concluding Rites

"Go in Peace, Glorifying the Lord by Your Life"

At a wedding I attended some years ago, a homeless woman entered the parish church just as the bride and the groom were preparing to serve as Eucharistic ministers. She came in through the back of the church and approached the altar. The whole assembly stopped and stared for a moment. What was going to happen?

The priest took the woman by the hands and introduced her to the bride and the groom. He sat with her, chatting, while the Communion Rites of the nuptial Mass unfolded. At the conclusion of the Mass, the woman, who had become the guest of the bride and the groom, joined the recessional line and walked out of the church with joy.

I have continued to reflect on this moment over the years. It serves as an icon of the closing moments of the Mass. We have heard the story of salvation, that narrative of love that is to make sense of our lives. We have received Christ's Body and Blood, becoming one with Love itself. And now we depart from our parish, blessed by the living God, to make a home for Love to dwell outside of our parish. In our cities, in our towns, in our rural village. We are to let the Mass bear fruit in our lives.

THE BLESSING

Most mornings, before I depart from home, I bless my son. I trace the sign of the cross on his forehead, praying that wherever he goes, God will be there with him. Praying that whoever meets his little toddler self will encounter God's love among them. I seal my blessing with a kiss on the forehead.

As we leave Mass, God blesses us too. Blessings before departure are important to the history of Israel. Jacob receives a blessing from his father right before Isaac dies—a blessing that passes on his birthright to Jacob. Moses receives a blessing from God which he passes on to Aaron and the priestly caste:

> The LORD bless you and keep you!
> The LORD let his face shine upon you, and be
>   gracious to you!
> The LORD look upon you kindly and give you
>   peace! (Nm 6:24–26)

May God be with you wherever you go. May God smile upon you, give you grace, and the peace of the kingdom that is God's alone to give.

Blessings, in the end, are for departures. As we leave the church, the priest blesses us in the name of the Father, the Son, and the Holy Spirit. A longer version of a blessing is encouraged during Advent, Christmas, January 1, Epiphany, Good Friday, the Easter season, the Ascension, Pentecost, and occasionally during Ordinary Time. We are to bow our heads during this blessing, as a child presents him- or herself before a parent to receive a kiss. Every blessing asks for God's grace to be with us wherever we go, whatever we do.

Once again, this blessing testifies to the importance of time and space, of history and matter, of the world itself for the Catholic imagination. Everything can become holy because of the holiness of God that now dwells with his Church, heading out the doors of the parish church to the world.

THE DISMISSAL AND THE SANCTIFICATION OF THE WORLD

After attending to the Eucharistic Prayer and the Communion Rite, it may be surprising to see how short the dismissal is. It's almost as if the Church is saying, "Ok, you worshipped well. Now leave and do something to transform the cosmos." The priest or deacon may proclaim, "Go forth, the Mass is ended." Here, the priest is playing off the very name of the Mass itself: *Ite, missa est,* (go, the assembly is dismissed). There are also options that are a bit less terse. "Go and announce the Gospel of the Lord," as well as "Go in peace, glorifying the Lord by your life." In every case, our response is "Thanks be to God."

The dismissal makes clear that although Mass is over, although the Eucharist is done, there is still work to do. There is still the peace of God that must be made known to all the ends of the earth. There is still the glorification of the world itself that is possible because the Word became flesh. There is still a world to be loved and transformed through our self-giving love in imitation of Christ's sacrifice.

It is the Mass that frees us to love as foolishly as this. To do the work of the Church in our families, in our cities, in our world. As Michael L. Gaudoin-Parker comments:

The Church is never a "finished" reality, but a reminder always of the pilgrim nature of human existence. Our attention is constantly directed ... in the Church's eucharistic celebration to realise our vocation or calling before the world as a people imbued with a deep, realistic sense of hope. The Eucharist commits us, in other words, to be responsible witnesses to the hope of eternal life, which contradicts the pessimism of the world's myopic time-bound preoccupations with materialism, productivity, success, etc. By celebrating the Eucharist we are schooled gradually to realise the truth for which Christ taught us to yearn: "thy will be done on earth as it is in heaven."[39]

We leave Mass with a job to do. This job is to sanctify everything in the world around us. As a father, this means that when I leave Mass I am called to love my son anew. As a husband, it means that I am called to recommit myself to my wife, to care for her with the very same love that Christ showed to the Church. As a teacher, it means that I am called to pray for my students, to soothe their anxieties, and to be tender in my corrections.

As a citizen of the United States, it means I am called to uphold the dignity of every human life from conception to natural death; it means that I am called to speak out against abortion, against injustices against prisoners, against the maltreatment of every immigrant. It means that I am called to offer hospitality to the poor and see each of these poor as the living image of Christ among us. It means that I need to work to end poverty through the renewal of society. It means that I'm called to invite my neighbor to come to Mass or a Scripture study with me, even if he or she isn't Catholic. It means that I am called to love.

It's not hard to find places in the world that need this Eucharistic love. It's not hard if we give ourselves over to a lifetime of worshipping at Mass, of practicing the art of self-giving love as we depart, and returning again to pray anew before the living God.

We can't transform the world on our own. We can't change laws that harm the unborn child or end racism on our own. We just can't. But we can stand before the living God, receiving his consoling and prophetic word, receive his living Body and Blood, and gain the courage to give just a bit more of ourselves away. To take the risk to love, even if it means our loss.

THE MASS AND MARTYRDOM

The icon of a Eucharistic life in the Church is the martyr. In the martyrdom of Polycarp, we hear about the transformation of the saint into a Eucharistic offering for the world:

> And when he [Polycarp] had concluded the Amen and finished his prayer, the men attending to the fire lighted it. And when the flame flashed forth, we saw a miracle, we to whom it was given to see. And we are preserved in order to relate to the rest what happened. For the fire made the shape of a vaulted chamber, like a ship's sail filled by the

wind, and made a wall around the body of
the martyr. And he was in the midst, not as
burning flesh, but as bread baking or as gold
and silver refined in a furnace. And we per-
ceived such a sweet aroma as the breath of
incense or some other precious spice.[40]

Looking through the horrors of this martyrdom,
the Christian can see this act of love as Eucharistic. Polycarp, worshipping God unto the end, even unto suffering
and death, becomes an image of Christ's Body and Blood
for us all.

That's the role of the saint. I will always remember
the last week of Pope St. John Paul II's life. In a world in
which the frail are dismissed for their lack of importance,
their lack of contribution to society, this holy man of God
died in public. He got sick in public, as we saw Parkin-
son's ravage his once athletic frame. He grew frail in public, as he gradually lost the ability to speak. And he died
in public, showing the entire world that the self-offering
of the Mass can transform even death itself. Eucharistic
love mattered to him unto the end.

For most of us, this is the kind of Eucharistic martyrdom that we will offer for the world—to testify to the
Eucharistic love at the heart of the Mass. A love in which
success and fame are less important than a life lived in
imitation of the Word made flesh. A love in which par-
enthood—and the sacrifices that come with having children—is actually the way toward human happiness. A
love in which we care for the sick and the dying because
they're Christ among us. A foolish love. God's love.

So at the end of Mass, go forth. Love your families. Love the poor. Love those on the margins. Love. When you do, you will begin to get a glimpse of what Revelation promises will be the worship of heavenly Jerusalem:

> Then I saw a new heaven and a new earth. The former heaven and the former earth had passed away, and the sea was no more. I also saw the holy city, a new Jerusalem, coming down out of heaven from God, prepared as a bride adorned for her husband. I heard a loud voice from the throne saying, "Behold, God's dwelling is with the human race. He will dwell with them and they will be his people and God himself will always be with them [as their God]. He will wipe every tear from their eyes, and there shall be no more death or mourning, wailing or pain, [for] the old order has passed away."
>
> The one who sat on the throne said, "Behold, I make all things new." (Rev 21:1–5)

The Mass will not always be the most exciting thing. It will not always lead us toward the height of emotion. Sometimes, it will just be a part of our lives, forming us in ways that we can't perceive.

Yet we go to Mass again and again, hopeful that God's construction project of our hearts will one day be finished. The result of this project will be the making of a saint—someone who will, when he or she dies, join the heavenly chorus of worship, rooting for the rest of humanity to join them in praise.

The Mass may be boring.
The Mass may not always be interesting.
But it is saving us.
It is sanctifying us.
It is our vocation.
Ite, missa est.
Go, the Mass is ended.
Go, renew the world.
Make me a disciple.
Go and make disciples.
Go.

QUESTIONS AND PRACTICES

1. Find a local Catholic Worker house of hospitality or other Catholic agency that does direct service to the poor. Volunteer there once a month, getting to know the guests. Pray for them at Mass.

2. Write a blessing for your child or a friend and pray it the next time you see him or her, either after departing or in the silence of your heart.

3. Think about where you live. Who in your area needs to experience the Eucharistic love of Christ? How might you share this love with those in need?